W9-BKG-089

FROM THE LIBRARY OF
THOMAS E. MASON. JR.
AN INFORMED VOTER AND CONCERNED CITIZEN
DEDICATED TO HELPING TIPTON THRIVE
DONATED TO THE PEOPLE OF TIPTON
WITH BEST WISHES FOR THEIR SUCCESS

DUFFY

DUFFY:
An Autobiography

Duffy Daugherty
with Dave Diles

1974

DOUBLEDAY & COMPANY, INC.
GARDEN CITY, NEW YORK

ACKNOWLEDGEMENTS

We gratefully acknowledge the generosity of the Department of Sports Information of Michigan State University, its director Fred Stabley and his assistant Nick Vista, who made the research not only possible but pleasant. A special word of thanks also is due Carolyn Rieker, who labored many hours with the transcripts of interviews. And without Francie and Danny and Dree Dougherty, and Beverly Susan and David Lisle Diles—who gave up time—none of this would have been possible.

The Authors

PHOTOGRAPH CREDITS
All Photos used courtesy Michigan State University Department of Sports Information.

ISBN: 0-385-05821-7
Library of Congress Catalog Card Number: 73-14044
Copyright © 1974 by Duffy Daugherty and Dave Diles
All Rights reserved
Printed in the United States of America.

DEDICATION

Of all the decisions involving the content of this book, the easiest to reach was to whom it would be dedicated. In reality, they are half dedications since this book, like our friendship, is a partnership. Duffy Daugherty wants his half dedicated to his wife, Francie, because she has been not only a beautiful wife but a lovely person who has given so much for so long. I dedicate my half to my late parents, Lisle and Lucille Diles, who gave me life, and to my beautiful children, Beverly and David, who give me a reason for living.

Dave Diles

There are some defeats more triumphant than victories.

Montaigne

Introduction

In recent years there has been a whole spate of sports books, many about football coaches. Personally, I have found most of them uninteresting, dull recitals of cliches and many of them so technical in a football sense as to be unreadable.

Not so with this book. It is fresh; it has style, taste and insight. Most of all, it is about a man who is at once interesting, full of humor and full of human concern. Through all the years Duffy Daugherty was more, far more, than a football coach. He has always been—above all—a family man and a man who cares about people. He has always, too, been an entertainer, a man who can tell stories for hours upon end and leave your ribs aching with laughter.

Somehow Dave Diles and Duffy have put it all together, have captured the essence of Duffy's spirit and Duffy's life. What emerges is not just another sports book, but a book that I think you will read, enjoy, and remember . . . and Duffy Daugherty deserves to be remembered!

Howard Cosell
February 13, 1974

Contents

The Day It Quit Being Fun

When we were called "The Alley Eleven" football was fun. Football in Barnesboro, Pennsylvania, always was fun. Thinking back, maybe it was fun because we won so much. Over one stretch we won twenty-seven in a row. We were just a bunch of grade school kids, but we had pretty good uniforms, and when we played all over Central Pennsylvania we drew good crowds.

Nutsy Fagan was our coach, but he really wasn't nuts. Matter of fact, he was a great coach and an inspirational guy. He really knew his football and the boys worked their fannies off for him. I remember one time he called the old sleeper play with one of our players lying down on one side of the field, hoping the other team wouldn't spot him. We had ten men in the huddle and the other team hadn't noticed our sleeper. A sure touchdown in the making!

All of a sudden the police chief of Barnesboro, an old English gentleman named Ellis Davies, came tearing onto the field yelling at the top of his lungs, "Stop the game, stop the game. There's a young man hurt over there."

It was terribly tragic at the time, but funny, too. I guess that pretty well describes football all over.

But one day, football quit being fun altogether for me and quitting became the only logical thing to do. I guess I first started thinking about quitting back in 1970. Maybe it's oversimplifying, but our Michigan State University teams weren't winning as often as I thought we should have, and winning had become more important than ever, and I didn't feel I could control the destiny of our Spartans. The faculty representatives of the Big Ten had placed so many restrictions on the coaches in our conference that it was impossible to compete on an equal level with the teams we had to play outside our conference. At my own school, neither the budget nor the facilities had kept pace with the teams we were supposed to beat right in our own league.

Getting beat by teams in the Big Eight, the Southeastern Conference and the Pacific Eight would never be a disgrace. The shame of it was we were getting our brains beat out because faculty representatives with their collective heads in nineteenth-century sand had taken away our weapons.

Perhaps I had been spoiled, too, by a tremendously favorable administration within the school. Dr. John Hannah was president of MSU from 1941 until 1969, and he was gung-ho for sports. His successor, Dr. Clifton R. Wharton, Jr., simply didn't have his finger on the pulse of the athletic program. I suppose he was too busy with other things, and I'm sure he underestimated the importance of a strong football program. And history proves that when victory becomes less important, victory becomes more infrequent. Administrative apathy, alumni despair, and coaching frustration—what a rotten trio that is!

Football was so uncomplicated when I was a kid growing up around Emeigh and Barnesboro, Pennsylvania. There weren't any elements that made you dislike the game. I loved it so much that I continued to play football even after I got out of high school. I went to work in the coal mines when I was eighteen years old and played football every Sunday for the Barnes A.C. team. Now, don't get me wrong. We didn't get paid for playing football. We got paid for working in the mines. But like I said, it was uncomplicated. I knew that if I didn't play football on Sunday, I didn't work in the mines.

You had to be tough, too, because we didn't have a lot of players. One time our coach talked a strong, young Italian fellow named Tony Mamone into joining the team. Tony didn't know anything about football. Matter of fact, he called it "foosball." But he was such a hulk of a man the coach figured he'd just put Tony on defense and have him take off when the ball was centered and grab the man with the ball. Tony had come over from Italy just a couple of years before, but he spoke excellent broken English.

Reluctantly, Tony Mamone joined the Barnes A.C. football team. He stood about six-feet-five and weighed in the neighborhood of 250, and we didn't have a uniform big enough for him. His jersey was too short and his knee pads hit him around the thighs. Tony joined the team the week before our game with the Portage Bulldogs. He didn't get into the game in the first half, but we had so many injuries he was pressed into service in the second half. We had to kick off, so the coach put Tony on the kickoff team and instructed him to get the man with the "foosball." Well sir, Tony went roaring down the field and one of those Portage Bulldogs blocked him and knocked him about ten feet into the air. Tony landed right on his face—and those were the days before face masks. He was out like a light and they hauled him off the field. Tony's mouth and nose were all bloody so they rushed him to the miners' hospital in the neighboring town, and there it was discovered that Tony had a broken jaw. They kept him knocked out while they wired his teeth together.

After the game, four or five of us drove over to see Tony and just as we got there, he was coming out of it. A doctor and a couple of nurses were in his room along with us when Tony discovered he could not open his mouth. The doctor explained to Tony what had happened and that it was necessary to wire his jaws shut so the bone in his left cheek could heal properly. The doctor explained to Tony that he'd have to be fed rectally, and somehow we explained to Tony what that meant.

He was furious. "How can I have spaghetti and meatballs?" he asked through clenched teeth.

The doc told him that for a few weeks, he'd have to stay on a liquid diet. Tony decided he wanted some hot chocolate, and he wanted it right that minute. So the nurse went downstairs and prepared a rectal feeding. In no more than five minutes she was back, hooked Tony up and began the process.

No sooner had the thing started when Tony was screaming and jumping around in the bed. The tube jerked loose and hot chocolate splashed all over the room.

"Was it too hot, Mr. Mamone?" the nurse asked.

Through his pained jaws Tony sputtered "No, too sweet."

Maybe things were too sweet too long at Michigan State while Dr. Hannah was president. I had hoped to coach a few more years, but when he left the downhill slide began. I always had the hope that when I decided to give up coaching, there would be other opportunities for me to continue some kind of association with football. It occurred to me that I couldn't wait any longer to begin a new career. So when we started the 1972 season I hadn't said a word to anybody, but I knew it would be my last season.

But somehow, as we got into fall practice, I got that old surge of optimism again, and I felt that even with all the restrictions placed on us Michigan State had a chance to be a title contender. We worked very hard to prepare ourselves for the opener, and we beat Illinois 24–0. It was one of the best opening games Michigan State had ever played. Illinois never got the ball past midfield. It was a game that should have been a tremendous confidence builder for a successful season because I've always felt a team makes its greatest improvement between the first and second games. But we didn't. Instead, we went downhill. Immediately we lost to Georgia Tech even though we had better personnel.

The blame? A piece of it goes to everybody. Obviously our staff didn't have our team ready, and I'm not sure I can understand why. Perhaps all of us had been demoralized by that time because of the limitations placed on us within the conference and the university and the sniping from the old grads. Then we took a slugging from Southern California. But my final decision didn't come until near the tail-end of the season, the Sunday following the Iowa game. We had had a season full of disappointment, and this was merely the final blow. We had lost a game to Michigan, even though we played well enough to win it, and deserved to win except for a couple of bad calls. As a matter of fact, this was the first time I ever received a call from the office of the commissioner telling me the films proved there had been some faulty calls, one that resulted in a touchdown being taken away from us, another that gave Michigan an undeserved score. I think the crush of the Michigan defeat carried over to the Iowa game, and we were tied by an inexperienced and inept football team.

First, I told my wife, Francie. Her reaction was predictable and beautiful. Whatever my decision, she'd stick with me. I told my staff on Sunday night, then talked with the squad on Monday. I called the players together after practice and as best I remember, this is what I said:

"This game is supposed to be fun, and I haven't succeeded in making it fun for you this year. I don't mean that practices should be all fun because there are certain parts of football that are sheer drudgery just because of the nature of the game. But Saturday afternoons, at least, should be fun. The fun comes from playing with zest and enthusiasm, and with feeling, then coming off the field knowing you have done your very best. A lot of the things you are required to do are not fun because they are foreign to your nature.

"Now, we've all heard people talk about players who 'love to hit,' and I've never known a decent football player who didn't love to hit. At the same time, I've never known a single player who loves to GET HIT. That's unnatural to want to have someone hit you. It's also a little goofy. But because football is the kind of game it is, a player has to condition his mind and his heart and his body to be willing to accept this kind of punishment for the good of the team. Now, say it's fourth and one. If some 175-pound running back is not willing to throw his body into a sea of humanity and get belted by a pair of 250-pound folks who don't like him, he'll never be able to play the game very well. But if that same runner tells you he likes getting hit like that, he's gonna wind up in a rubber room somewhere.

"Fun in football comes from doing things together as a team, having success as a team, and knowing you have played well and given the utmost of yourselves. This feeling transcends all else and is much more vital than individual accomplishment. Because I haven't been able to make football fun for you fellows, I am resigning at the end of the 1972 season. But from now until the end of the season, by God, it's gonna be fun! Now, we play Purdue on Saturday. Purdue is a big, tough team, and if we're gonna win on Saturday, we're gonna have to walk with a growl all week."

Then I told the players that there's a whole heap of difference being tough, and appearing to be tough.

"You guys might look tough with those muscles rippling through those MSU T-shirts, but you haven't been playing tough."

For my part in making things fun again, I promised them one joke each day before practice and on that Monday I tried to emphasize the difference between looking tough and really being tough. I told them the story about the cowboy who tied his horse outside the saloon and swaggered into the bar for a couple of shots of red eye. When he came back outside, someone had painted his horse's balls purple. He checked to make sure his six-guns were loaded, hitched up his gun belt, and when he made his way back through the swinging doors his jaw was more firm, his step more confident. His voice was heavy with rage when he finally spoke, standing squarely in the center of the barroom:

"O.K., where's the clown who did the paint job on my horse? Stand up and take your punishment like a man."

Well sir, one guy stood up. Matter of fact, it seemed like he'd never quit getting up. He had about 280 pounds spread over his six-foot-eight frame and he bellowed right back at the cowboy,

"I painted your horse. Whaddaya gonna do about it, shrimp?"

The cowboy quickly dropped his hands away from his pistols and meekly sputtered, "I just thought I'd tell you the first coat is just about dry."

I don't know if it was the jokes, or the squad's relief that I was finally leaving, but we had short but spirited practices all week. We practiced with enthusiasm, and when Saturday came we played the same way, defeating the favored Boilermakers 22–12.

After my decision to quit, I spoke with athletic director, Burt Smith, and with Jack Breslin, the very powerful executive vice-president of Michigan State University. I spoke frankly with both and told them there was a lot of work to do before State could again become competitive, even in the Big Ten. Years ago, our facilities were considered tops in the Big Ten, but the year I left we were just about at the bottom. Our salaries for the coaching staff were ninth lowest in the league, and we didn't even have a meeting room in which to show movies to the squad. The only school with a lesser budget was Northwestern.

I wanted to put all the disappointment and frustration behind me if I could, and make the rest of the season a pleasant experience for everyone. Naturally, the gentlemen of the media were very kind to me. But I know a fellow always has nice things said about him at a wake, too.

We not only beat Purdue, but went out the following Saturday and upset mighty Ohio State. But in the Purdue game, we had missed two short field goals plus an extra point, and I made up my mind the following week to

change kickers. Our new man was Dirk Krijt. He was a
foreign student, from The Netherlands, plus he was a
walk-on.

We had already played a couple of games before I met
him. He just came walking up to me at practice one day and
asked if I were the coach. I told this slender young man
with shoulder-length hair that there were differences of
opinion about that. It turns out he had never seen a football
game, and didn't even know what a touchdown was. He
told me he had played soccer, though, and wanted to see if
he could kick the football. We got him into a sweat suit,
some soccer-style shoes and hauled a sack of footballs to
one end of the field. And he could kick, all right. I decided
to put him with the junior varsity to give him some game
experience, but he didn't get much because that team
didn't score much, either. But right before the Ohio State
game we elevated him to the varsity, and his name wasn't
even on the program the day of the game. But everyone
knew him after the game. Dirk Krijt had kicked four field
goals in the first half, a Big Ten record, plus an extra point.
We won the game 19–12 in a tremendous upset. The
Spartans, everyone said, had not only won one for Duffy,
but two.

We had unusually heavy press coverage and a lot of
media people were interviewing me in the locker room.
Dirk strolled by, and he was smoking a cigarette. I acted
like I didn't notice him, but Dirk made sure I did. He
walked right up to me and said, "Coach, I'm gonna go out
tonight and celebrate with a girl and have a few beers. You
wanna come along?"

Somehow I still held out a flicker of hope that no one
would recognize him as our hero. Maybe they'd take him

for one of our equipment people. I couldn't have been that lucky. One of the sharper newspapermen asked if that wasn't our kicker. Even at that stage of my career, I knew when I was totally trapped and so I mumbled something like, "Matter of fact, I guess that might be him."

Then came the questions about our training rules at Michigan State—cigarettes, booze, and broads. My reply was quick, if not satisfactory to the Women's Christian Temperance Union.

"We have a new rule," I announced sharply. "Anyone who can kick four field goals in one game is allowed to do most anything he likes."

But conditioning is the one thing a coach rarely has to worry about. Players who aren't in shape play themselves out of the line-up, and the gifted athlete makes proper conditioning a part of his everyday life.

Dirk now has completed his studies at Michigan State and returned to his home in Europe. When he left school, he made some strong comments about American football, saying people take it far too seriously and that it is a violent game that reflects the American way of life. I suppose lots of people can make a case for that, because football is not an activity for the weak and the timid. But competition is the thing that made America great. Really, it's the reason there is an America. And I am persuaded that those who engage in spirited, even heated competition derive things that others may never be able to understand. There is something truly beautiful about getting down on your hands and knees and digging and scraping for something that you really want, even if it's something like one simple victory. When you accomplish something like that as a part of a team effort, there are few things more gratifying.

It is sweat and sacrifice, it is pain and punishment, it is grit and guts, and it is fun. And when I told our players the week before the Purdue game that it had not been fun the way it was intended to be, I told them the story of the married man whose idea of fun was to go out drinking with the boys. His wife didn't think that was fun at all, since she was staying home taking care of the children. Finally, after years of putting up with this sort of thing, she gave him an emphatic warning that if he came home boozed up after midnight just once more, she'd march right to the lawyer's office. She wasn't the kind of woman to make idle threats, so he took it as more of a promise.

For three or four months, he was on his good behavior. Finally, though, he couldn't stand it any longer, and he got roaring drunk. It was nearly four in the morning when he stumbled home. He was crawling up the stairs, his shoes off, trying to keep from waking her up. On the wall at the stair landing, they had a coo-coo clock. The damned thing started blaring out its four A.M. message. He had the presence of mind that comes only from being an experienced drinker, so he blurted out eight more coo-coos himself, figuring that if she heard the clock, she'd think it was midnight instead of four A.M. He managed to get into bed without arousing anyone and when he made it down to breakfast next morning she was smiling and greeted him with a cheery, "Good morning, hon."

She gave him a peck on the cheek as he sat down to his favorite breakfast of buckwheat cakes and sausage. As he got ready to leave for work—convinced he had gotten away with his escapade—she wondered if he'd have time to drop off the coo-coo clock for repairs, and he wanted to know the trouble with it.

"Well, during the night," she said, "the thing coo-cooed four times, belched, broke wind, said, 'O shit' and coo-cooed eight more times."

Life always has been fun for me. As a child in the rolling hills of Pennsylvania, things were simple and uncomplicated. My dad worked in the mines, later ran the company store and later went into business for himself in a clothing establishment. I guess the toughest decision I had to make in those days was selecting which chicken we were going to eat on Sunday. When I was just a little tyke I raised chickens in our back yard. I guess I had fifty or sixty of them, and I had names for each one. I really loved them and it choked me all up every time Mom would decide to fix chicken. I couldn't decide whether she should fix Janice or Lucy. The truth was, I would have preferred that we never ate chicken.

I recall fishing in the streams around Cambria County, and later on I worked in the mines. I remember singing that old song, "My Sweetheart's a Mule in the Mine."

Sports was a major part of my childhood. My father had been an exceptional athlete and so were my two older brothers. From the time I was in grade school, I knew I wanted sports to be a part of my life, although I had no idea I could ever make that dream come true. My dad used to tell us boys that he used to practice his tackling by jumping over a coal cart after rats. It was considered a sloppy tackle unless you got the rat by both hind legs.

For about ten years, no one except a Daugherty played center on the Barnesboro High School football team. I remember going to see a college game at Pitt in 1934. The Panthers played Minnesota, and that was the only game

Pitt lost and Minnesota went on to win the national championship. That was two years after I graduated from high school. I skipped the sixth grade so I got out of high school when I was sixteen. I worked as a special delivery boy and in a bakery shop, and in those days I didn't think much about going to college. Maybe it was so remote I didn't dare. After high school, I worked two years in the Phillips-Jones Shirt Factory, then two years in the coal mines at Arcadia.

I had to get up at 4:30 A.M. and then drive thirteen miles to the mine. We had to get our powder and supplies and be inside the mine working by 6 A.M. I guess there were two hundred men working in the mine, and we worked in three-man crews. Since we worked in a low vein, we had to wear pads and work on our hands and knees. Before long I figured out there must be a better way to put bread on the table.

Those were the days when I was playing football every Sunday against top semi-pro teams around Pennsylvania. Even though we didn't get any money for it, we played with more zest and determination than some of today's athletes making $100,000 a year.

One day, a fellow named Jim Rorapaugh saw me play. He had gone to Syracuse, and he recommended me to that school and to Coach Vic Hansen. Oddly, I didn't get an athletic scholarship. I got an academic scholarship because I had good grades in high school. I should have. After all, my father was president of the school board! I agreed to go to Syracuse without having seen the campus. I had seven dollars in my pocket when I set out hitchhiking the 350 miles. Vic coached just my freshman year, then Ossie Solem took over. Biggie Munn was the line coach and my good buddy Bud Wilkinson was the quarterback coach. Matter of fact, the first dinner his wife Mary ever cooked was for me and a couple of other football players they had over. Little wonder that Bud and I have been so close over the years.

My college playing career was interesting even if Walter Camp didn't know whether I was on foot or horseback. I got to start my first game as a sophomore, and that season we gave Colgate its only defeat. I broke my neck my junior year in a game against Penn State, but played another game or two after that before missing the final game of the year. I played my senior year and was elected captain of the team.

I had majored in finance and was offered some jobs after graduating from Syracuse, but war was imminent and I had my heart set on being an Air Force pilot. I went on a crash diet and lost twenty pounds—then flunked the eye test. So I stuck around Syracuse and coached the line for the freshman team in 1940 then went into the Army and did some coaching in Texas before going overseas. I was no hero, but in twenty-seven months I learned some things about life and about myself. Strangely, I think my experiences in New Guinea helped hone my sense of humor. The Australian soldiers, perhaps because they had been through so much, used to laugh at our being so scared. I was so embarrassed, and they were so strong. So I started laughing through the bombings and strafings. Right then, I knew if I could laugh at all that, I could laugh the rest of my life, no matter what.

I had gotten married right before I went overseas. It was what you might call a whirlwind courtship. I had met a lovely girl named Francie Steccati in San Francisco. We met on June 8, on a night when I had a blind date with another girl, but Francie and I talked so much the other girl got mad and left. Francie and I were married nineteen days later.

After the war, Biggie offered me a job on his staff at Syracuse. The job paid $2,000 a year, and the next year I followed him to Michigan State and got a $1,500 raise. From then, through the 1972 season, it was mostly fun. It was fun at Syracuse, just as it had been fun on the sand-lots and in the hills of Pennsylvania. I spent seven years on Biggie's staff at MSU before getting a chance to be a head coach. That experience lasted nineteen years. Like I said, most of it—I'd say 95 per cent of it—was fun. But the other 5 per cent made me gag.

Men Are Four

Men are four: He who knows not, and knows not he knows not, he is a fool, shun him; he who knows not, and knows he knows not, he is simple, teach him; he who knows and knows not he knows, he is asleep, wake him; he who knows and knows he knows, he is wise, follow him!

For years the Big Ten has had its head in the sand. For a long time the Big Ten was the pride of the nation in football, but through neglect and indifference let its football teams become second-rate performers.

The men who have been in control of Big Ten sports, for the most part, are mid-Victorian thinkers. Some aren't thinkers at all.

Faculty representatives simply aren't qualified to run athletic programs. It was always stupid to see great football people like Fritz Crisler, Biggie Munn, Red Mackey, Ivy Williamson, and Stu Holcomb sitting around powerless to control the destiny of the sport they helped build to such gigantic proportions. Their hands were tied when it came to making decisions that really mattered. That's because the Big Ten really isn't the Big Ten. It's called the "Western Intercollegiate Athletic Association of Faculty Representatives"—that's the official title, and the faculty folks have taken great delight in letting people know they were in charge. These men, I'm sure, are fine men in their own fields. Trouble is, their fields are science and mathematics and economics and law, not sports. All the time we had these other men, the athletic directors, who had devoted their lives to the conduct and administration of athletics, and they wound up being nothing more than hand shakers and hand wringers, watching on the sidelines, powerless as their conference went down the drain as a first-class sports power. It's the same thing as putting caddies in charge of golf greens. For the most part, the faculty representatives lacked two things—vision and courage.

Their refusal to allow the five-year or red-shirt rule and their restricting the number of scholarships and their acceptance of that ridiculous need factor proved beyond all doubt their total lack of knowledge of modern-day football. Only through the dedication of hard-working coaches has the Big Ten not slipped totally out of sight. Over the years, the Big Ten built its reputation on its success against non-conference opponents. In recent years the same conference lost 75 to 80 per cent of those same games. It's surely no coincidence when you lose twenty-one straight to teams from the Big Eight.

We didn't lose any at Michigan State because we had the good sense not to schedule teams from the Big Eight. But we didn't have sense enough to avoid Southern California and Notre Dame and some others. It's simply not fair to coaches to force them to get along with half the number of players, who have one year less to mature. I've never been able to understand why the Big Ten felt it was intellectually superior to conferences like the Big Eight, the Southeastern, the Southwest, and the Pac-Eight. We surely proved we weren't physically superior. What happened was tragic, and unnecessary. What would happen was this: A pretty good Big Ten team would have to play two or three of those tough schools and they would be outmanned. By the time you got to your conference schedule, your record would be tarnished, along with your image. It would hurt your team emotionally and physically, rob your schedule of some of its luster. By that time, you could very well have lost the enthusiasm of your players and the support of your students and other fans. How in the name of sense could you sell it, when one team had played Colorado and Nebraska, the other Southern Cal and Missouri, then the teams with 0–2 records go out and play each other? It simply didn't mean a great deal to the alumni, the students, and the news media if you went out and hammered Indiana after losing your first two games.

In 1972 our three non-conference opponents were Georgia Tech, Southern California, and Notre Dame (on successive weekends, yet!) and at a banquet that fall attended by MSU president, Dr. Clifton R. Wharton, Jr., I pointed out that he held degrees from three universities— Harvard, Johns Hopkins, and Chicago. I wondered out loud why in the hell he couldn't get those three alma maters on our schedule.

This sort of trouble fell on all of us in the Big Ten. Well, almost all of us anyway. Some of our coaches had more compassionate athletic directors and they scheduled teams like TCU, Virginia, Navy, and Duke. I always thought it would have been nice to play teams like that because they operated pretty much the way we did, and we'd have had at least an even chance to win.

For many years, our faculty representative has been Dr. John Fuzak. I had more than a few run-ins with him over these mounting problems, but I never got the feeling he war really listening to me. I argued with him about the archaic rules under which we were forced to operate and his answer was always the same. To operate under the rules that governed other conferences would make us less academic. Then I'd always ask him to name a Big Ten school that was academically better than Stanford or California or UCLA. That always stopped him, but it never changed his mind. I guess there's truth in the old adage that there is none so blind as he who WILL not see.

Big Ten coaches had their hands tied, and more often than not their mouths gagged all because a small group of men with little knowledge and understanding of the program wanted to throw their weight around and prove that they were really running the Big Ten. And the coaches had to go out and beat the bushes and beg some seventeen-year-old kid to come to a Big Ten school because of its proud tradition for football excellence. It's like trying to convince a man he should fight alongside you even though the whole world knows you're running low on ammunition.

I told every young man who played football at Michigan State that he need not put on a uniform if he didn't plan to have fun. But I'll tell you, defeat is no laughing matter, and it's an even more bitter pill to swallow when you know you didn't have as much of a chance to win as your opponent.

Time and again, our coaches would come up with unanimous recommendations. We'd take our case to the athletic directors, and most of the time they'd agree with us. They in turn would take the issue to the faculty representatives, and they'd inevitably vote it down. If it meant progress, if

it meant joining the twentieth century, if it meant moderni-
zation and streamlining, it was dead. In my nineteen seasons
as head coach, communication between faculty representatives and coaches and athletic directors was almost non-
existent, and in all that time we had but one joint meeting.
Even then, nothing was accomplished because the faculty
people came into the meeting with their minds already
made up. For example, I remember how we pushed to have
our freshmen report at the same time with our varsity, but
it was repeatedly voted down. We'd give grants-in-aid,
then deprive the young men of the opportunity to learn our
system.

For what seemed like centuries, they voted for the no-
repeat rule, arguing it was scholastically disruptive for a
team to go to the Rose Bowl twice in succession. But the
faculty representatives went out to Pasadena year after year,
with all expenses paid. Apparently it would have disrupted
studying, but not teaching. Another thing that really got
under my skin was in the one joint meeting we had, after
all the issues had been discussed and recommendations
brought in, when it came time to vote, the faculty reps
asked everyone else to leave the room. Even now that the
red-shirt rule has been approved and scholarship grants are
equally distributed and the no-repeat rule has been re-
scinded, it'll take the Big Ten another year or two to begin
regaining some of its lost prestige. It should be obvious to
everyone that in the Big Ten the job of athletic director
isn't much. It requires no real decision-making ability. The
athletic directors make schedules but have no final
authority on rules and regulations that really matter.

It's no accident that Southern Cal and Texas and
Alabama are among the top teams in the country year after

year. John McKay, Darrell Royal, and Bear Bryant—all
very good friends of mine—operate strong programs with
the approval and understanding of a friendly administration,
and their hands aren't tied down by a bunch of old fogies.
The ideal situation is to be both coach and athletic director
in a strong conference that operates with up-to-date
theories and practices.

Did you ever hear of a president getting fired for an
inadequate athletic program? Mostly, they want strong
programs that are financially successful (and that means
winning) because they have alumni to please, stadia to fill,
and contributions to acquire. Good as the biology and
education departments might be, not many old grads use
them as rallying points. Call an alumni meeting to hear a
speech by someone from the geology or English department, and the only way they can get a crowd is if the guy
shows X-rated movies. But get the football coach out to
talk about his upcoming team, and you'll turn 'em away.
In recent years the Big Ten coach has had to get up and
face hostile crowds and try to explain how he lost to a team
from the Big Eight and another outfit from the Southwest.
And it's safe to say that only a small fraction of the old
grads understand that the coach had an administrator who
wanted to win within the rules, a conference that made it
impossible to compete on equal footing, a faculty rep who
figured winning too much was a sin, an athletic director
who was helpless, and a press that never could understand
why you didn't go 10–0 every season.

In 1965 I was speaking to an alumni group and several
times I referred to "my team" and "my squad" and so
forth. Then I caught myself:

"I'm sorry, this team went through the season unbeaten

and untied. This is YOUR team. Now, last year's team won
four and lost five. THAT was MY team." They laughed,
but I'm not certain they really thought it was funny.

I guess I should never had been hurt or surprised by
anything after 1961. We won seven and lost two that
season, beat Michigan and Notre Dame, and yielded only
50 points all year long. Yet, after the final game, I was
hanged in effigy. God forbid that I should ever be forced
to occupy the same foxhole with the kind of person who
would do something like that. That kind has tapioca for
guts!

In 1958, we failed to win a single conference game, but
the thing that hurt most was a critical letter I got from an
old grad. It wasn't his choice of words, but I objected most
to the fact that the letter arrived promptly on my desk and
the only address on the envelope was "Duffy the Dope."

But most members of the media and most alumni were
understanding. But in the later years the critics became a
heavy cross, and once in a while their disappointment took
violent forms.

I recall one alumni meeting that began with a golf
outing and ended with a rather late dinner. I was in the
midst of my talk, naturally telling about the prospects for
the upcoming season, when suddenly some drunk yelled
out from the back of the room, "Hey, Duff, how many
niggers are you gonna start this season?"

I'm sure I've never been madder in my life.

"First," I said, "before I answer the question, if the clown
who asked it is man enough to come up here, I will do my
very best to punch him in the nose."

He didn't make another peep and maybe that was a
good break for me. But the room fell silent, before I went

on to explain that it was my policy to play the best players, whether they happened to be all black or all white. I've never made the color of a man's skin a consideration. But we had a lot of people who regularly and generously supported our scholarship program. On one occasion one of these gentlemen hosted a party at his home and Francie and I went. Before we really got going, the host said to me, "Duffy, you've been using a lot of niggers lately. You know, the minute you start four of them in the same backfield, you've lost me."

I looked this man straight in the eye and said, "Then, I've lost you right now." Those are the last words I've ever spoken to him. I told Francie to get her coat, and we left. We've never been back to his home and what's more, we never will be, no matter what.

When I started at Michigan State, I had thirty or forty people around me, and I'm proud to say that the same group was with me when I left. Maybe I should have tried to enlarge the group, but coaching is too time-consuming to maintain close contacts with very many people, sometimes even one's own family. Not a single member of this group ever became disenchanted with me as a coach. They understood the problems while some others never tried to. It's like the pinch hitter who was sent up to bat with the tying run on third base, and one out. He needed only a decent fly ball to bring in the tying score, but instead he took a called third strike. He just couldn't pull the trigger, he was totally fooled on the pitch. When he came back to the dugout the manager was furious.

"Jesus, don't you realize we're paying you $30,000 a year to hit guys like that?"

"You're damned right I know that," the batter snorted

back. "But don't you realize the other team is paying that pitcher $40,000 to get guys like me out?"

Just as being coach and general manager of a professional football team is an ideal situation, it is better in college for one man to be both coach and athletic director. The format has proven successful—give a man both jobs, a good administrative assistant to handle some detail work, some encouragement from upstairs, rules he can live with, and this man can win.

I enjoyed some success, but there are no secrets to success. I had no magic formula, and neither does anyone else. There are certain problems that are unique to football and they really can't be put in a bag with every other sports activity on campus. Let's face it, in ninety-nine cases out of a hundred, football supports all the other athletic endeavors. If a coach isn't also the athletic director, he then should have the opportunity of going to the president or to a top administration official whenever problems arise.

When Andy Gustafson was on the staff of Colonel Earl Blaik at West Point, Andy had a chance to take the job at Miami of Florida. Naturally he consulted with Coach Blaik, and the old redhead gave him just one piece of advice: Make sure you're responsible ONLY to the president of the university.

That was the beauty of my job at Michigan State for so many years. Dr. Hannah was president of MSU for twenty-eight years, and he saw it grow from a so-called cow college of 7,000 students to its present-day enrollment of more than 40,000. He saw Michigan State gain acceptance in the Big Ten and grow in every possible way. He truly loved the school and he had but one desire—to make Michigan

State the greatest university in the world. He had his finger
on the pulse of every department and wanted the school
to excel in every area. He just couldn't stand to be second-
best in anything.

Most of all, this man was a realist. He wanted everybody
around him to join in the pursuit of excellence, but he
didn't expect you to accomplish miracles with mirrors so
he gave you the tools with which to work.

We'd meet frequently, I'd tell him what the problems
were and what we should do to correct them, and he'd
invariably say, "O.K., Duff, this is the way it'll be. I know
you're not going to abuse your position."

He'd rely on my judgment. We never really had to
worry about a budget when he was president. As soon as
he left, everything changed. Now, don't get the idea that
John Hannah was some frustrated jock. He's a brilliant
man who has served in high government offices under a
handful of presidents of both political persuasions. He may
be the wisest man I've ever known. Because he was a realist,
he recognized obstacles to perfection. But because he was
an idealist, he still wanted to strive for it. When Biggie
Munn recommended that I succeed him shortly after
MSU's Rose Bowl victory over UCLA *in January 1954,* there
was a three-way meeting involving Biggie, myself, and Dr.
Hannah. Dr. Hannah was worried because it was going to
be only our second year in the Big Ten, and a lot of people
still thought of us as a cow college (I guess some folks still
do). I remember him saying:

"It's a rugged conference. If you can win one more than
half your games, you'll be doing a great job. But I'd rather
have you beat Michigan and Notre Dame more than they
beat you." I'm certain that's one yardstick by which he

measured me, and fortunately we came out on top against both of them, losing seven times in nineteen seasons to each team. There was a stretch of eight years where we didn't lose to either one.

Dr. Hannah was a unique man and I'm sure there haven't been many administrators like him. I'm just as certain there were times when I disappointed him, but he was never openly critical. And he was a most persuasive man, and there were several times when he talked me out of other jobs I might have taken had it not been for his influence. I like to think that by nature I'm a loyal person, and I always realized that he took a chance on me when no one else was beating at my door. When other opportunities came up, I never used them as a wedge for more money or a better deal. But more than once, Dr. Hannah got me aside for heart-to-heart chats. He told me I was important, not just to the football program but to the university. Anyone who tells you he doesn't like to hear things like that is a liar or a fool. You know, there were times when Dr. Hannah came very close to thinking I was as great as I thought I was.

Every coach gets criticism because no one wins them all, but I can truthfully say that Dr. Hannah's support more than made up for any harpoons sent my way. When he left I felt as though a big support pillar had been removed from my very foundation.

Strong football programs—and let me make it clear that I'm all for them—are inevitably backed by strong administrations. If you're going to successfully compete in the big time, you must have not only the sympathy and interest but the support of your administration. It just won't work any other way.

I made up my mind this book wasn't going to be a bitter

attack on the game of football nor the people in it. I owe all that I have to football, but the book has to be honest, too. And it is a fact that while John Hannah was president, we had gung-ho interest and aggressive support from the top. All that good stuff disappeared when he left in 1969. In all fairness to his successor, it should be pointed out that Dr. Wharton arrived at a hairy time. There was a lot of student unrest across the country and a lot of pressing social problems. Because Dr. Wharton didn't understand football's great impact he tried to delegate responsibility to others. One of the things he delegated was the responsibility for the football program. The man simply didn't understand the vitality of the program, nor its needs.

I hung on as coach for three seasons after he took office. When I left after the '72 season, our athletic budget was ninth lowest in the conference. Dr. Hannah just wouldn't have let that happen.

Some of my favorite dinosaurs served on the NCAA Football Rules Committee. Someone once described a camel as a horse built by a committee. The rules committee forever has been dominated by men no longer active in coaching. They're out of touch and out of step. They were great in their time, but their time largely had passed. I'm not saying they weren't conscientious, but it's possible for someone to be conscientious and stupid at the same time.

Every time I think of the rules committee, I think of an old man I once met in a bar. He was shaking with palsy and his entire body trembled so much he could barely raise his drink to his lips without spilling it all over hell's half acre.

"What are doing these days, Fred?" I asked.

"Same old racket," he replied. "Brain surgery."

The NCAA Rules Committee simply refused to let the game remain under the same set of rules. They changed the rules like some schools change coaches. For example, the substitution rule was changed eighteen years in a row. Imagine that! Pure nonsense.

College coaches would meet each year, and our conventions always were held in places like Chicago or New York. We have a coaches' rules committee, and all the coaches send in their recommendations. For example, we might vote 4 to 1 for free substitution, or 5 to 1 for putting the goal post back on the goal line. Later on, the rules committee named by the NCAA would go to some classy place like Hawaii or Florida and meet for another week. They'd consider the recommendations handed them by coaches or athletic directors. They'd sit around and debate the issues for a week, just to justify that dandy trip. I guess they felt required to make some changes in the rules after such a vacation.

One year, they came up with a ridiculous rule that a player could make only two appearances a quarter. That meant that if you started a game and came out, you could go back in just once, no matter what. A couple of Big Ten coaches simply ignored the rule and when we brought it to their attention that they were cheating, they just shrugged. Matter of fact, one coach said, "What do you expect me to do? I don't have a good backup quarterback, and I couldn't put my Number One guy back in for fear of getting him banged up on defense."

One year, the coaches voted overwhelmingly to put the goal posts, or at least the cross bar, back on the goal line. Years ago, that's where they were and before the posts were padded there were a couple of fatalities, so the posts were moved ten yards off the field of play as a safety factor. But why should the game be played on a field 120 yards long as far as the kicking game is concerned? So the coaches recommended moving the uprights out to the goal line, using a cantilever device to keep the post out of the way. But the big wheels on the rules committee couldn't see things our way. After all, we were just modern-day coaches. What did we know about the game? The old dinosaurs' explanation was that such a change would be too expensive for a lot of the smaller schools because they'd have to have special goal posts built. Right up to then, that made sense.

Then, in the next breath, the rules committee decreed that the goal posts should be widened from the then 16 feet to 18 feet. They must have figured every school had post stretchers. So everyone—small schools included— had to rush out and build new goal posts anyway. Now that was a typical, not an extraordinary, decision.

For years, the game was governed by four officials on the field. In some cases, though, the coaches felt they weren't getting enough coverage. The field judge could handle one sideline for out-of-bounds plays, but it was difficult for the head linesman to get downfield for a deep pass. Besides, he didn't get all the proper mechanics of coverage on certain downfield plays. We felt the need for more coverage on things like pass interference and so there was considerable sentiment for a fifth official. We named a committee to report back with a recommendation to the rules committee. We indeed recommended a fifth official and a redefinition of responsibilities to create better football for players and fans. After that, we argued about a name for the fifth official. Among the suggestions were sub-umpire or No. 2

linesman, but after considerable bickering, Jimmy Aiken, who was coaching at Oregon then, stopped everyone cold:

"Why don't we just call him sonofabitch, because that's what he'll be anyway."

All coaches respect officials. It's just that we recognize them as human beings capable of making mistakes. I've had my share of run-ins with them, and in one particular game I was having a running feud with a specific official. I thought he was having an atrocious day, and I told him so. I was yelling out something to our team, and he started pacing off a penalty. When I asked what it was all about, he yelled back, "Five yards, Daugherty, for coaching from the sidelines."

Now I had him cold. "That shows just how stupid you are," I barked. "Coaching from the sidelines is a fifteen-yard penalty."

He walked over and put a warm hand on my shoulder and informed me that for the kind of coaching I was doing, it was only five yards.

The old AP writer, Fritz Howell, used to tell the story of the coach and the referee who had been at each others' throats all afternoon, and after one particular five-yard penalty the coach called out, "Ref, you stink."

The referee promptly stepped off another fifteen and yelled back, "How do I smell from here, smart aleck?"

In general, I think officials do a good job under difficult circumstances, but sometimes you'll run into one who makes himself more conspicuous than the game. It's the trademark of a good official to operate in almost total anonymity.

Before he coached at Stanford, Jack Curtice was at Texas Western and one time down there he had a running back who started so quickly off the snap that he was always being called for being in motion. Early in one game the guy went sixty-three yards for a touchdown but the officials called it back—backfield in motion, they said. In the second period he goes thirty-five more for another score and bang, it's called back for the same infraction. Curtice is fuming. Comes the second half, and his man rips off a forty-six-yard touchdown run and for the third time, down goes the flag and back comes the football. Jack can't contain himself any longer. By the time the referee has stepped off the penalty, Jack is nose-to-nose with him and questioning his ancestry. Naturally, he gets fifteen more for unsportsmanlike conduct, but Jack isn't through screaming.

"I don't care if you step off a hundred and fifteen yards," he screams, "but I'll guarantee you the films will bear me out—this young man is not in motion. He just starts so quickly it LOOKS like he's in motion."

The referee looks straight in Jack's face and calmly says, "Cool off, Jack. I didn't penalize him for backfield in motion. I penalized the other ten guys on your team for delay of game."

Psychology and Other Weapons

The greatest tragedy—and perhaps "tragedy" is too strong a word when we're talking about the outcome of a football game—but the greatest disappointment of my coaching career happened on New Year's Day of 1966 in the Rose Bowl against UCLA. When I quit coaching, I was asked to name my ten most memorable games. I listed all defeats and some folks thought that was odd. Some felt it was too much negative thinking on my part, and perhaps it was. But defeats stay with you a lot longer than the victories, especially when they are defeats that are snatched from the jaws of victory. Some games really got down and dug at the pit of my belly, and I still think of them sometimes.

I read somewhere that a coach described defeat as being worse than death because you have to live with defeat. I can't buy that, but defeat is a painful thing, particularly when it had no business happening.

Later on in this book I'll go into the ten most memorable games in detail because I think in some of them, anyway, the psychological outweighed the physical.

The late Vince Lombardi said football was 75 per cent psychological. I've never taken time to break it down into

percentages, but mental attitude is very important. By
that, I mean the physically better team does not always win.
And I've never seen a team do well if it's not mentally and
emotionally prepared to play. And things are not always on
the surface. Through the years, I can think of many little
items apparently of no significance at the time and far
removed from the field of play, but they turned out to be
things that caused great triumphs or brought on crushing
defeats.

I'm sure there is a spirit in college football that you don't
find in the professional ranks. Still, those emotional locker-
room orations are overrated. Matter of fact, they don't
occur as often as the movies would have us think. And it's
a rare thing when a newspaperman's article posted on the
locker-room wall will inspire a mediocre team to victory
over a superior foe. Like the old gentleman from
Stratford-on-Avon said, the play's the thing.

I remember a fine young quarterback named Pete Smith,
and he became our quarterback by accident. He had been
a pretty good high school player at Ecorse, Michigan, but
he wasn't the type of kid you'd go out and beg on your
hands and knees to come to Michigan State. Pete was what
we call a walk-on. He didn't come to school on an athletic
scholarship. More often than not, a walk-on walks out
unnoticed three or four days after walking on.

But Pete became very important to us. We had recruited
two good quarterbacks the year before, but both of them
got big bonus contracts in baseball and that left our
freshman team without a recruited quarterback. So Pete
was it. He weighed 165 pounds and he didn't have intimi-
dating strength. At a banquet, you might mistake him for
a bus boy.

So Pete started the first game of his junior year simply because we didn't have anybody else. We beat Wisconsin 20–0. The next week, we defeated Stanford rather handily, but in the middle of the game, Pete's father died. He was in the stands at East Lansing. The funeral was scheduled for the following Thursday so, naturally, Pete went home for the entire week. It was the week prior to our all-important game against Michigan, and I cannot describe the mood of our practices that week. Hardly anyone spoke. Pete had said he would be back on Thursday following the services, so we held the start of practice up half an hour. We had been working quite a while when Pete came onto the field. Everyone saw him, and the young quarterback who had been running the first string offense in Pete's absence simply trotted over to the other side, as if to say, "O.K., Pete, here's your job back."

The players still were quiet when Pete went into the huddle. When he finally looked at them, all he said was, "I didn't come back here to lose to Michigan."

Pete played the most inspired game I've ever seen anyone play. He did nothing you could call spectacular, but here was a young man with what you'd honestly have to call ordinary ability, and he reached deep down within himself that afternoon on Michigan's field before 103,198 fans and led the Spartans to a 28–0 victory. One of our touchdowns came on a pass he threw to Carl Charon.

We had a similar thing happen with the Saul twins, who played so well for us in the late 1960s. The night before a game against Wisconsin, I was informed their father had died. It was my duty to break the sad news to the boys. They talked with their mother, then came back and informed me they had decided to stay and play the game before going home to be with their mother. She had given them her blessing to do it. Those young men played with a motivation that could have never come from a pep rally or a dressing-room talk. We won that game handily, too. I think—in fact I know—that an entire team boosts itself up to a great emotional height when one of its members finds himself in deep waters.

In November of 1963, the whole world was terribly shaken by the tragic assassination of President John F. Kennedy. We were scheduled to play Illinois the following day. We were undefeated in the conference, so the championship of the Big Ten and the trip to the Rose Bowl hung in the balance. Our players were at home, so they watched television and got the full impact of the tragedy. The Illinois players didn't know about the whole thing until their plane landed in East Lansing. Now, our players were geared to give the most of their God-given talents and skills, we were peaked to an emotional pitch and ready to dedicate all that we had to our late President. Our men were anxious to show love of country and President. But the game was called off just an hour before the kickoff, and finally played five days later. Pete Elliott had told me that his team was so shocked it couldn't possibly have done a decent job.

The postponement had an effect on both teams. Our guys were so charged up I took them out for an hour's workout just to let off steam. By the time the game got underway the following Thursday, Illinois was high as a kite and our guys couldn't find their fannies with both hands. We committed seven turnovers and got our ears pinned back 13-0. Illinois went to the Rose Bowl and I watched it on television in disgust.

Prior to our 1968 game against Notre Dame, I told members of the news corps that I was seriously thinking about opening the game with an on-side kick. I guess no one took me seriously. At least the Irish didn't. But that's exactly what we did, we recovered the ball and went on to upset Notre Dame 21–17.

Sometimes a joke can turn the emotion and as a consequence the predicted result of a game around. One time in the late 1950s one of our linemen—a married fellow with a houseful of children—got caught carrying a big box of cereal out of a dormitory. I'm not saying he was stealing. He just suddenly found this big box in his arms and he neglected to put it down where it belonged. The team knew all about it, because things like that are difficult to conceal (apparently about as difficult as a huge box of cereal). We were getting ready for our traditional game with Michigan and we had come up flat. I needed something to give our guys a little spark.

Most of the time, you don't need any contrived situations when you're going to play Michigan or Notre Dame. Generally, our guys were so high we'd have to shake the trees to get them to come down for practice. But this week was an exception. So I set up a deal with my pal Sheriff Bill Barnes.

The following afternoon, he roared onto the practice field in his patrol car. The siren was blaring and the lights were flashing and our kids were scared half out of their wits. Matter of fact, some of our coaches were shaking a little, too, and I've always wondered why. The sheriff came right to the point.

"I'm here to pick up one of your players, coach," he barked, and he went on to explain that he had a warrant for the arrest of this particular fellow. One of our assistant coaches stormed at the sheriff and a lot of pushing and shoving ensued. I figured it was time for me to step in so I blew several times on my whistle to try and restore some order. By this time every man on the team was ready to fight, and I could just see the headlines. I pleaded with the sheriff.

"You can't take him now," I begged. "This is the week of the Michigan game. If you'll just release him to my custody until after Saturday's game, we'll see what we can do to get this mess straightened around. I'll see to it that he behaves and doesn't leave town, and I'll turn him over to you after the game."

Sheriff Barnes couldn't have been more co-operative.

"I'll go you one better, coach," he said. "If you beat hell out of Michigan, I'll drop the charges."

Well, that lightened things up considerably, the practice was breezy and fun again, and two days later we went out and kicked the daylights out of Michigan.

We have had some great battles, particularly with Michigan and Notre Dame, and I'm sure their people have worked just as hard to come up with some little gimmick that might provide a psychological edge. They say that the great Fritz Crisler of Michigan employed one tactic over and over again. The locker rooms in Michigan Stadium are right across the aisle from each other and Crisler used to leave the Michigan door cracked open a bit. He'd wait until the opposing team was about halfway out onto the field, with half the squad still sauntering out of the dressing room, then he'd release his Michigan players and they'd come out yelling like maniacs and going a hundred miles an hour down the tunnel onto the field. Time after time, the other team would move aside and let the mighty men of Michigan pass by. They were thus intimidated before the game ever began. Of course, most of Fritz Crisler's teams were powerful enough to intimidate you without any gimmickry.

In 1963, we had a fine team led by Sherman Lewis. On the morning of our game at home against Notre Dame, I went to church with the Catholic members of our squad. Services were held at the Student Center. On this particular day, the Notre Dame players had asked if they could have their mass at the same time as we had planned ours. Being a gracious host, I told them to use the center altar.

I had recruited a good friend, a priest from Ireland, to say mass for us at the side altar. Of course, Notre Dame brought a lot of priests. They had offensive priests, defensive priests, priests in charge of fumbles and interceptions, you name it. We finished at about the same time, and one of their priests told the Notre Dame players he had a relic of Ste. Bernadette and that they could come up and kiss it. Our guys weren't invited to take part, so they just sort of stood around looking into space.

I thought it might have unnerved some of our guys, so later on I informed them that the Feast of Our Lady of Lourdes is not until the month of February, and that since this was only November, the Notre Dame boys were a few months ahead of blessing time. Besides, Bernadette was accepted into sainthood because she helped the afflicted, and so only the afflicted should prevail upon her for assistance. I told our fine young men they were healthy and strong and perfectly capable of taking care of themselves without any outside help.

Well, Notre Dame got off to a 7–0 lead, and led 7–6

until little Sherman Lewis shook loose for the winning touchdown, going eighty-five yards with less than two minutes to play. I don't think his speed was impeded by the Ste. Bernadette medal I gave him to wear around his neck.

I've never believed you can win a game through a last-minute appeal nor with some super-inspirational message seconds before kickoff. And a proper mental attitude just doesn't come overnight. You have to work on it all year, and let's face it, each squad has a different set of emotional gears. You're dealing with a team, but a team is a collection of individuals. And you have to know these people, one by one. When you're recruiting, you have to separate the young men with genuine interest in you and your school from the kid who's just shopping around seeing how many free trips he can get.

If a boy is merely shopping—no matter how good he might be—it's smart to lose interest in him right away. I always figured I'd have trouble getting a young man like that to concentrate. The individual relationship within the framework of a team is one of the genuine joys of coaching. In football, or in anything else in life, every human being has a button. It's up to the coach to find out what motivates a particular boy, you have to find the button. Now, you don't always find it but you have to try, and I think you sometimes try even harder with the young man who is more difficult to reach.

I remember that before our 1956 game against Notre Dame, we had a lousy week in practice. We were rated No. 1 in both the wire service polls, and I'll confess we were a little cocky. After all, we were the defending Big Ten champions and we had won the Rose Bowl game. We were

favored to defeat Notre Dame but this was a good Notre
Dame team, as all of them are. It was Paul Hornung's senior
year and Jim Morse was their captain. We knew Notre
Dame would be sky-high, and all the coaches tried to warn
our guys that this was no ordinary team they would be
playing. Besides, we were playing at South Bend, and
winning there is like trying to pass abortion legislation in
Rome.

We had beaten Stanford, Michigan, and Indiana and
were coming off a 53-point production against Indiana.

The Fighting Irish announced plans to bring back all
the living Notre Dame All-Americans to see the game, to
resurrect the memory of the immortals, Knute Rockne and
George Gipp.

When we got to South Bend for our Friday afternoon
workout, a whole batch of legendary figures surrounded
the field to watch. The Four Horsemen were there, so were
Hart and Lujack and a ton of others. Our players were
bug-eyed and you could hear them telling each other, "That
big guy over there smoking the pipe is Leon Hart" . . .
"Hey, the Four Horsemen are standing over there at the
40-yard line" . . . "That's Johnny Lujack over there talking
to Angelo Bertelli." A strange, quiet mood descended
over our entire squad. Ordinarily, our Friday workouts are
relaxed and lots of fun with jokes all around. But not this
time. The eerie mood continued all through dinner, even
through the shoot-em-up movie we brought along to show
the players.

We had our hot chocolate and cookies (in later years we
also provided Hawaiian punch as a gesture to our players
from Hawaii) and still hardly a word was uttered. I knew
right then we were in a heap of trouble, and I didn't know

what the dickens to do about it. I talked it over with the other coaches and they were puzzled, too.

Finally, next morning at our pre-game meeting I told a few of my funnier stories and nobody even snickered. And that's unforgivable. So I tried the shock treatment. I told them they weren't ready to play, weren't concentrating on the game, weren't thinking properly, and that this Notre Dame team was gonna run them right out of the stadium. I ranted and raved and stormed around and still they didn't budge.

If I wasn't effective, I was at least prophetic because Notre Dame came out with a great rush and in about half a dozen plays went into our end zone and quickly took a 7–0 lead. Luckily, we got a couple of breaks and scored on a plunge by Pat Wilson and tied the game, but they out-played us so badly they could have been ahead by three or four touchdowns. Finally, with just three or four minutes left in the half, they were on our 30-yard line and Hornung went back to pass. Jim Morse was all alone in the end zone but Clarence Peaks, surely one of the greatest athletes I've ever seen, leaped about five feet into the air and not only batted the ball into the air, but ran into the corner of the end zone and caught it for an interception.

I was beside myself. Here we were, the top team in the country, barely holding on for a tie. Peaks had run the ball out to the 22, but we were set back to the 7-yard line for clipping. I was grateful we weren't being run out of the ball park, so I ordered our quarterback to run Peaks into the line three times, hoping we could get a first down, run out the clock and try and regroup at half time. On the first play, Peaks ran over about seven Notre Dame players and went ninety-three yards, but the touchdown was called back for clipping. Finally we had to punt. Our center, John Matsko, centered the ball all of eighteen inches. It was the queerest thing I've ever seen. He just sort of dribbled the ball back and Notre Dame got it and went storming down the field. They were at our 7 when the half ended. We dragged ourselves off the field looking like anything but the No. 1 college football team in the land.

Forget all that junk you've heard about half-time orations. Normally, you spend most of your time making technical adjustments, trying to pinpoint the things you've been doing well offensively, sticking to things that have been working and throwing out the things that have flopped. Sometimes you add a little something. But on this day, I knew our problem was not one of a technical nature. So, for the first five minutes, I did nothing but pace up and down in front of the squad. I couldn't believe it! The players were still in that trance! They really believed that garbage about winning one for the Gipper. They slumped on their chairs, heads bowed like whipped pups. Finally I turned to our captain, little Johnny Matsko, and asked, "John, what in the name of sense happened on that pass from center?"

John was in a stupor. "I honestly don't know, coach. It was as if someone had his hands on that football."

"C'mon, John," I pleaded, "don't bring the supernatural into this thing."

Just then, our second-string center, Don Berger, piped up. "Hey, maybe it was old George Gipp reaching up to put his hand on the football."

"Don't be sacrilegious," I cautioned. "Maybe it was George Gipp reaching DOWN."

Well, that broke the ice. Finally, someone had found the

button for the entire team. I didn't want to spoil the mood, but I gave the guys just a little talk.

"Don't you fellows realize how foolish you've been? You've been caught under the spell of the Golden Dome. The Good Lord has far more important things to attend to than the outcome of a football game, even if one of the teams is from Notre Dame."

Then I got the players together in a circle and told them they could tell any joke they wanted. So we sat around and swapped stories and one of our players got so wrapped up telling this long, drawn-out story that we nearly got penalized for being late for the second-half kickoff. In fact, we were warned. But the story was worth waiting for, and when our guys came out of the tunnel they were laughing hysterically. The fans must have thought we all were nuts, but we had a tremendous load lifted from our shoulders, and we went out and scored 40 points in the second half and won the game 47–14. It will always stick out in my memory as the greatest single-half performance I've ever seen in football.

And it was nothing more than a mental block that influenced the whole afternoon. That game had more psychological impact than any other game in which I've participated.

If a coach could just figure out the key to unlock every young man on his squad, and learn how to motivate him to a supreme effort every time he steps onto the field, then bottle it, he'd be a billionaire. By the same token, I've seen teams go flat, and nearly gone mad trying to figure why.

In 1961, we had won five in a row and had given up just 10 points in decisively defeating Wisconsin, Stanford, Michigan, Notre Dame, and Indiana. We had beaten

Michigan 28–0. Michigan had beaten Minnesota 41–0. And
Minnesota blanked the Spartans 13–0, and to this day I
can't explain why we were so flat. I know we weren't ready
for the game, and it's such a helpless feeling. It's terrible to
know that a team is not emotionally ready to play a game,
and at the same time feel you've done all that you can to get
the team ready. I don't think George Gipp or Amos Alonzo
Stagg or Bronko Nagurski or Jim Thorpe or anyone else
ever reaches down or up or in or out and puts his hand on
a football, but I do think there are times when you simply
aren't meant to win.

Like the game against Illinois in 1956. We had just come
off that great second-half effort at Notre Dame, yet we got
knocked off by an Illinois team that our second stringers
would have beaten on a normal day. We were far superior
to Illinois physically, but when we got down to Champaign-
Urbana the students and alumni were riding herd on Coach
Ray Eliot. They had strung "Goodbye Ray" signs all over
the campus. Perhaps some of the students didn't like Ray,
but his players surely did. They whacked us good, 13–0,
Abe Woodson had a great day, and we came back home
with our tails between our legs.

We were bigger and stronger and faster than Illinois, but
that day their players just wanted to win more than ours
did.

This sort of thing happens to teams, and it happens to
individuals. For one reason or another, a player can get
himself up to a peak he may never be able to reach again.
There is a magic button that when pushed inspires a man to
a performance out of all proportion to his physical
abilities.

Dennis Mendyk comes to mind in this area. He was a

sturdy and capable running back who was steady but not
sensational. He was our top ground gainer in 1956, caught
a few passes, intercepted three passes, did some punting,
was our top kick-return man, and led the team in scoring.
Still, he peaked for just one game, and it was that day
when we roared in the second half against the Irish.

Dennis had come from a relatively small Catholic high
school in Michigan and like many Catholic players his
dream was to attend Notre Dame and play football in the
shadow of the Golden Dome. But Notre Dame didn't
recruit him, so he came to Michigan State. And he might
never have become a regular for us had Walt Kowalczyk
not been injured. Dennis Mendyk scored our go-ahead
touchdown against Notre Dame on a thirty-eight-yard run
and later ran sixty-seven yards for another score. He later
told me he had carried this determination with him for a
long time, and it gnawed at him, this being snubbed by
Notre Dame. He just wanted to prove to the folks at Notre
Dame they had made a mistake in not giving him an
athletic scholarship. It was the finest day of his career.

I'm certain similar things have happened to people in
every avenue of life. I know it has happened to coaches, who
because of some added incentive or because a mission was
created within the inner man, achieved a level of success
that might otherwise have escaped them. Necessity may be
the mother of invention, but without opportunity, there is
no chance to show what you can do. And without an
overpowering challenge, life often becomes dull and there
can be no mind-boggling success.

Like I said, I'm sure the Good Lord doesn't really care
who wins football games. If I felt otherwise, I'd have
scheduled practices for the church lawn. It bothers me that

some coaches seem to be using religion as a weapon. To me, religion is a very private thing. I have nothing against conducting a prayer session before games if the coach is prayerful and religious by habit. But it smacks of the worst kind of hypocrisy for a coach who never darkens a church door to use that sort of stuff as a gimmick.

In my nineteen seasons as a head coach, I considered religion a personal thing involving a player and his God. We avoided religious gimmickry. Instead, we had a minute of silence before each game. I felt that if there were players who wanted to pray, this gave them that opportunity. For the others, they could at least collect their thoughts or whatever they wanted to do. After all, that one minute belonged to them. The rest belonged to Michigan State.

As for myself, I always prayed silently for the wisdom to do the right thing, for the players to do their best, and for the men on both sides to escape injury. I thought that was about as generous as I wanted to get—and I'd like to think that a few of the opposing coaches once in a while did the same thing for my players.

And all that junk about football being a character-building thing is just that—junk. Character is built in the home and in the church, not on a football field.

An old coach told me it'd be interesting if we had an all-star game between Heaven and Hell. Those up above would look down and say, "We're gonna win because we have all the good players."

But those down below would be every bit as confident of victory because they'd have all the coaches and referees.

Recruiting and Other Demons

The Big Ten Conference forced its football coaches to cheat. And today, by any yardstick you want to use, recruiting is dirtier than ever before. Now, any time you're dealing with human beings, especially when there is something at stake, you'll run into some wrongdoing. And as long as there has been recruiting—in sports, industry, and in every other human endeavor—there have been rules violations.

I'm like every other coach in the world. All any of us ever want is a fair advantage. Not every coach is totally honest and there are no degrees of honesty. Either you're honest or you're not. It's like trying to be a little bit pregnant. The idiotic rules we've had over the years in college football forced coaches to cheat and to lie. We had some recruiting violations at Michigan State when I was an assistant coach and we were put on probation for a couple of years. Our violation was one of stupidity because we weren't charged with going out and buying our players at so much per pound. What we did, we did openly. A bunch of downtown people formed the Spartan Club, and each member pitched in a hundred dollars a year, sometimes more, and the money was to be used to pay room and board and tuition for our athletes. It was determined that some of the folks who were getting the money weren't qualified for it.

We had another problem in 1959 during the time I was the head coach. I found out there had been some rules violations, but I took the matter before the infractions committee myself. I was the one who turned Michigan State over to the authorities because I found out that some of our players were getting aid to which they were not entitled. I immediately put in a call to the then commissioner, Bill Reed. I told him the situation had been corrected. It involved just one coach who was recruiting in one area, and he had arranged for some players to get extra financial help.

There was a time when every coach in the Big Ten admitted to cheating. It wasn't merely widespread, it was unanimous. It happened during the so-called "need factor" era. I thought at the time that whole concept was stupid, and I've never had reason to change my thinking on it. Need should be based on how badly the young man needed an education, not on how badly the school needed a quarterback. The concept seems complicated, but perhaps I can explain it simply.

To qualify for room, board, and tuition, a young man needed to come out to what they called "zero computation." The boy's family was required to submit a financial state-ment based on income. From that would come the determination of how much help the young man could be given. Say, for example, the figure came out to $900. If it cost $1,200 to go to school, you then could give the prospect $300. The ideal situation was to get everything to come out to $000.00, and the whole mess was so complicated and fouled up that everyone was cheating on the computations.

We finally all went to Commissioner Bill Reed and openly admitted we all were cheating. He said at the time that if he could get us to promise not to give anything more than room, board, tuition, and books, he'd help us get rid of the need factor. He did, and it was a great day for the Big Ten when it was all over and done with. It was just another of the rules that tied our hands and helped cost the Big Ten its supremacy in football. It didn't have a single positive aspect to it.

We've been mired in the Stone Age as far as red-shirting and the transfer and junior college rules and all that are concerned. Our administrators tied the hands of the coaches, then wondered why we got our brains beat out by the Big Eight and other more enlightened conferences. Why would a young man pay to go to Michigan State or Iowa or Purdue, when he could go to Colorado or Nebraska or Texas or Alabama or Southern Cal for nothing, and get some financial aid to boot?

Kids seventeen and eighteen may be impressionable, some may be conniving little devils and some may even be a little slow to catch on, but they all can count. I learned a tough lesson in the mid-sixties when our first-string center, Walt Forman, quit football after his junior year because his nearly perfect point average in the classroom won him immediate admission to medical school. I decided right then and there I'd never again recruit a player that intelligent.

The AP's Fritz Howell (an early mentor of my co-author) said he could remember the days when a triple threat was a guy who could run, pass, and kick—instead of one who was being paid by the school, the alumni, and the downtown coaches. Fritz always had a good memory.

No question about it, I've seen some ugly and flagrant abuses over the years, but considering the hundreds of thousands of young men who have been recruited to play the game, the abuses have been relatively few in number.

Ohio State's Woody Hayes said not long ago that recruiting is more bitter and dirty than he's ever seen it, and Woody had some harsh words for coaches and administrators who fail to honor contracts. He thinks we ought to have tighter rules on recruiting. That would be fine if the rules were uniform nationwide.

When a coach is hired, he must understand that he has one job, and that's to fill the stadium. You don't fill it by losing. Winning is the name of the game, and it's an unwritten understanding between the coach and the man who hires him: Win, but don't you dare get caught cheating. You know if you do get caught, you're going to lose your job and you're going to find that you're all alone out there. The administrator will turn his back on you, the faculty representative will say, "I told you so," and the athletic director will deny knowing anything about it. As for the alumni, they're rubbing their hands waiting for another coach to second-guess.

The Michigan State grads are like all others—they're with the coach, win or tie!

The various booster organizations are well-intentioned, but their members naturally feel they can do a better job than the coach. That's precisely why they're car salesmen and office managers. Once in a while, despite their good intentions, they've been known to make life pretty miserable for a coach. A coaching friend of mine got fired, after several underwhelming seasons. All during his career, he had faithfully gone to the Downtown Coaches' meeting each Monday noon, and there he would explain the loss on the previous Saturday and try to provide an optimistic outlook for the upcoming game. When he got canned, he asked the president of the boosters' organization if he could make one final, farewell appearance before the group. The president figured that was the least they could do for him, and doing the least for him was in keeping with the nature of the organization. When the deposed coach stood up, here's what he had to say:

"I didn't get up here to say good-by, because that's so final. I didn't come here to say so long, because I don't want you jerks to think I ever want to see you again. I don't want to say au revoir, aloha, or sayonaro because you're all too stupid to understand that, but as I turn and walk out the door, you'll get the general idea of what I'm trying to say by the sprig of mistletoe hanging from my coattail."

Old grads are the same everywhere. They want so badly for their team to do well. They want to be able to brag about it, and to say, "that's my team." But when you finish 5–4 on the season, it's always the coach's team, not the alumni.

For a long time at Michigan State, we had the students, the fans, and the alumni baffled. John Kobs always had good baseball teams, Biggie and I got 'em accustomed to success in football, and Pete Newell gave our basketball program new life. Now I see where Pete is tremendously upset by what he sees in the colleges. He's now general manager of the Los Angeles Lakers of the National Basketball Association and listen to his strong words:

"It's tragic to hear a college coach say, 'I can't be in the top ten unless I cheat.' I've heard it too many times from men I respect and it's a helluva indictment. If that's the case, there's something terribly wrong. A lot of coaches lose their jobs because they haven't won and a lot of them lose their jobs because of illegal recruiting. But I've never seen a college president lose his job for doing either one. It's vicious. One coach takes advantage of the rules and another coach is fired because he loses too many games."

A successful football program is important to a major university. Surveys prove that there is a direct correlation between winning and alumni contributions. When you win, the old grads are more generous. So all of this puts the pressure right on the coach, and he in turn places it on the young men who are playing the game. And it all starts with recruiting. When we were fortunate enough to win it all and go to the Rose Bowl, we had alumni coming out of the woodwork. Everyone who ever came through the Student Union felt he was entitled to four tickets on the 50-yard line. I always said it was a good thing we didn't go to the Rose Bowl more often. That way, I kept the disgruntled alumni to a minimum.

Recruiting always has been tough, but when I first began coaching, it at least was halfway sensible. We had only to compete against Michigan and sometimes Notre Dame for the top prospects in the state of Michigan. Later on, the premium on winning became so great, recruiting so widespread and sophisticated, our rules so restrictive, that we found ourselves competing with dozens and dozens of major colleges and universities. Everyone was out doing whatever he could to place the prospect under obligation. Once you start doing this, you've opened the floodgates. It can lead to anything, and it did just that. If a prospect was naïve, chances are his father wasn't, and he'd start pitting one school against another and the ugly element of greed would take command. Sometimes I felt the fathers of high school seniors were better negotiators for their sons than the agents for the professionals are today.

There's cheating today, but it's usually slickly done and it's difficult to pin a violation on a coach or a school. Your regulatory agencies such as the NCAA and the various conferences realized a long time ago they could not police all the alumni activities, and it's tough to get the evidence if someone wants to do something special for a good prospect. And there's so much jealousy among schools and coaches that the out-and-out cheater knows if he wins big, he'll be examined not as strongly by the NCAA as by the other coaches and schools right in his own conference.

I can't say that I didn't like recruiting. I did, for the most part. I liked visiting with folks and explaining what I considered to be advantages of Michigan State. I never once tried to sell a young man on the basis of education. Let's face it, you can get pretty much the same education at every school in the country.

What griped me most was this business of apparently having a young man all set to attend Michigan State, then finding out that the following weekend he's off on a visit to another school, and the next weekend to still another school. Some kids have traveled more as high school seniors than the editors of *National Geographic*. So you had to keep going back, time and time again, trying to persuade some seventeen-year-old to come to your school. Perhaps you never knew, but you always wondered about the tactics being used, and you had to wonder if the rules weren't being broken.

I don't suppose we'll ever settle the argument about whether a very successful football program is a help or a hindrance to recruiting. We think we used it to good advantage, because the blue-chip athlete knows he's going to play and he wants to participate in a good program. Other schools use this as an argument against you. Their favorite line is, "You don't want to go to Ohio State or Alabama. After all, they have a ton of good football players and you'll wind up sitting on the bench. Come with us, and you'll be certain to play."

The one thing I learned in years of recruiting is that mothers have far greater influence over a boy's decision than fathers. The dads always like to think the boy will go to the school his dad selects, but time and again the mother would be the final influencing factor. Our staff was acutely aware of this in our glory years, and sometimes I think they recruited on the basis of beauty (or lack of it) among the mothers. We used to jokingly pick a "Mother of the Year" with honors going to the prettiest mom. Let's be honest about it—when you're recruiting kids seventeen and eighteen years old, their mothers probably are in their late thirties or early forties, just in the full bloom of life. Sometimes our coaches might have overlooked a good tackler, but they never ever missed a beautiful mother. Ofttimes when it came to select our "Mother of the Year" some of our coaches would have two, even three candidates. I'll tell you, the competition was fierce.

I knew a coach at a school in the Northwest who was recruiting the son of a very attractive divorcee. In his efforts to persuade the young man to come to his school, he spent considerable time and effort wining and dining the mother. Of course, he was single and being on the road recruiting didn't work as much of a hardship on him as it did some other staff members. He and the pretty young thing wound up on more than one occasion, parked out by the reservoir in back of town. When it finally came down to the time for signing the letter of intent, she wrote the coach a letter explaining that her son had decided to attend school at Houston, but SHE was coming to his school for some work on her master's degree.

Many times I've faced fathers who'd say, "Well, coach, I'll think it over and I'll let you know what we decide." In the background there'd be the mother with that knowing smile on her face, because she already knew where their son would be going to school.

Recruiting can be fun but it's always hard work. We worked diligently to convince parents that Michigan State was the right school. We'd invite parents to the campus and make it a point to know about the young man's academic background, religious affiliation, and hobbies, and we had outstanding co-operation on campus while Dr. Hannah was president. It was heartbreaking to work so hard on a blue-chip athlete, feel in your mind he was all set to attend your school, then see him make a last-minute decision to go somewhere else. If he did well elsewhere, it at least was good to know your evaluation of the talent was on target.

Competing against Michigan was a great challenge, because the school enjoyed a tradition of excellence in sports and in the classroom. Michigan folks called us a "cow college," and we had our own little pet names for them, too.

I was on a plane one time and the two men across the aisle from me were talking football. It wasn't a matter of eavesdropping, rather I simply couldn't avoid overhearing what they were saying. They were arguing about a particular rule in football, so I quietly volunteered the information that settled their mild dispute. Then I went on to talk with them for a while.

I told the fellow occupying the window seat that my guess was he was from Michigan State. He affirmed that and wondered how I knew. I told him that Michigan State men carry themselves with a certain amount of dignity and quiet confidence, that his conversation indicated a good vocabulary and an excellent educational background, that in general the way he conducted himself led me to believe that he had been a graduate of Michigan State. He was quite pleased at my perception. Then I turned to the fellow in the aisle seat.

"And I'll just bet you're a Michigan man."

By golly, he was just that, and he wanted to know how I could tell.

"I noticed the 'M' on your ring as you were picking your nose!"

Good athletes stick out just like that. It does no good to tell them they'll never get a chance to play. There's something about the innate bearing of a truly superior athlete that another fellow never has. Maybe it's a feeling of confidence way down deep, but fellows like Clarence Peaks and Brad Van Pelt and Gene Washington and Joe DeLamielleure and George Webster and Walt Kowalczyk —when they walked onto the practice field they had something extra going for them.

There's tremendous competition for these young men. But once in a while, you'll get a non-recruited walk-on who sticks out. Such a young man walked into my office one day. I just looked up and there stood this Adonis. He even had to stoop down a bit to make it under the door without hitting his head.

"May I talk with you, coach?" Hell, I would have suited him up if I had to send him to Berlitz to learn English. On looks alone, the cheerleaders would have paid his tuition. We shook hands and I thought my arm would fall off. He had a grip like a boa constrictor. I doubt that I have ever seen a finer physical specimen. He must've been six feet five and weighed about 220. There wasn't an ounce of fat on him. He had blue eyes and blond hair. He looked like I always thought I did until they invented mirrors. I wanted him to sign a tender right then and there. Even if he couldn't play a lick of football, he'd make an outstanding son-in-law. Think of the beautiful grandchildren he'd create!

He told me that all he wanted to do in life was to play football for me and Michigan State. It was, he said, his lifelong ambition. I asked him to sit down, and he unraveled this story:

"When I was a freshman in high school, I wasn't too big —only six-one and barely 180 pounds—so I played flanker. I caught 19 touchdown passes and scored 11 other touchdowns. I carried six times on the end-around play and six of 'em went for touchdowns. I did all the punting, averaging 41.7 yards a kick and I hit on 37 out of 37 extra point tries. Oh, I nearly forgot, I kicked nine field goals.

"As a sophomore, the regular quarterback got hurt so they moved me into his spot. I'd never played there before but I guess I did all right considering my inexperience. I threw 26 touchdown passes, but they still let me run some, and I averaged 9.6 yards a carry on 102 tries. Of course, I continued to do our team's kicking but my leg cramped up on me in the fourth game, and it really never came around so my punting average slipped to 40.3.

"I guess you could say I came into my own in my junior year. I played quarterback on offense and linebacker on defense. I guess I had about 130 unassisted tackles, and for the first time in the school's history I was named most valuable player on both offense and defense. My arm was a little sore early in the season because I had pitched baseball all summer, but I still managed to complete 93 out of 127 passes. I threw for 17 touchdowns and ran for 16 more. My speed seemed to pick up a little that year and I averaged about 13 yards a carry.

"We really put it all together in my senior year. Only three teams scored on us and we won the league title for the fourth year running and the state Class A championship for the third straight year. Individually, I guess you'd say I had a pretty fair season. I was all-state for the third time. I was really happy I didn't have to play defense. I was really bushed by the time the season was over. I had something like 30 touchdowns, half running and half passing. My kicking was better, though. Got my punting mark up to 44.8.

"We were so far ahead in most of the games I didn't try but five field goals. Made all of them, though. I ran my string of extra points to 116 before the holder fumbled a pass from center in the next-to-last game and the kick sorta squibbed off to the right. But then, records never meant anything to me. They're made to be broken, I figure."

I couldn't believe my ears. It was like finding out that Raquel Welch is smart, too. I asked the fine specimen if he played other sports and he told me:

"Like I said, coach, I played baseball. High school ball was sorta dull, even though I hit .571 through my career and won 48 straight as a pitcher. Those high school kids don't have very good fastballs and they'll hang curves on you all the time. Sand-lot ball was a lot more fun because I got to play against guys in college. The competition was a lot tougher, and it showed in my batting average. I hit only .488 against those older guys.

"Played basketball, too. Center and forward. All-state for two years. Guess I averaged something like 38 points a game in my varsity career."

I was almost afraid to ask if there was anything else. I even got up and closed the door in case there was a Michigan spy lurking around. The kid continued:

"I fooled around with track but actually there wasn't much time because I had to fit track in between baseball and football. I did run the dash and hold the state record for the hundred, but I had to run in my pads because I came straight from football practice."

Right about now, I couldn't have cared if this kid had the ugliest mother in captivity. I would have rented a mom for him or paid for plastic surgery for the one he already had. I could visualize him out there on a crisp autumn afternoon, tearing through Notre Dame for six and seven yards at a crack, catching a dozen passes against Michigan, firing through to dump the UCLA quarterback for an eleven-yard loss, intercepting a pass against Georgia Tech, throwing three touchdown passes against Ohio State. The only problem I could foresee was figuring out where to play him.

We'll foul that up later, I thought. Trick is, get him to

sign a tender, then get him in school. My God, does he qualify academically?

Reluctantly, I asked about his grades. "I suppose with all those sports activities you didn't have much time to hit the books?"

His face dropped. Nervously he shuffled his feet.

"Don't worry about it," I tried to console him. "If you're a little short, we have people here who can help you."

Finally he spoke. "I knew you'd discover my Achilles heel. My grades really aren't what they should be. It's true, I hardly ever studied. Seems like all I did in high school was play. I finished up with a 3.8 point average and some girl with a 3.9 beat me out for valedictorian."

Staggering! Absolutely beautiful! Not only is this kid the greatest athlete I've ever encountered, but an honor student to boot. My palms were already sweaty as I fumbled through my desk drawer for a tender for him to sign. As I searched for it, I told him, "You know, you're the finest prospect I've ever encountered. It's gonna be a lot of fun to have you here at Michigan State. But tell me, don't you have one tiny, little weakness anywhere, one chink in your armor, one fault that would sort of bring you down to the level of other young men your age?"

"Just one, coach," he confessed. "I AM inclined to lie a little."

The name of the game is WIN. Coaches must understand one basic thing: The stadium was built to be occupied. If Lady Godiva rode into a stadium today, she wouldn't pull half the crowd that we get for the Michigan State-Michigan game. People just aren't that interested in looking at white horses. If you fill your stadium just for graduation exercises, that can mean only that you've paid your commencement speaker far too much money.

Because of this unbelievable pressure to win, coaches are forced to go to great lengths to recruit the blue-chip athletes. When coaches are interviewed for head coaching jobs and the administration spokesman says the school wants a "representative" program, that means you're supposed to win your conference championship. If he says you're supposed to be "competitive," it means you are supposed to place well up in the national polls. If you are told the school expects you to produce a "rewarding" athletic program, that means you are supposed to get invited to a bowl game every year. If the man talks about the institution's "proud tradition," that means don't buy a house and don't put on any long-playing records. This is why most coaches rent.

Some coaching jobs have more built-in hazards than others. I knew, for example, my main job was to beat Michigan and Notre Dame. Alabama's Bear Bryant knows he's not supposed to lose to Auburn. John McKay would lose brownie points if he loses to UCLA. I understood my hazards—at least the ones I could see.

It's been overwritten and overreported about the ingenuity and inventiveness of coaches. In the pros, I suppose, Hank Stram of Kansas City and Tom Landry of Dallas are regarded as two of the more creative people. In the colleges, much of a coach's creativity comes in recruiting. If you don't get the good talent, all the genius in the world won't make you win. So many great stories have been passed on through the years that sometimes we tend to think of them as exaggerations, if not outright lies. But most of them are true.

For example, the late Peahead Walker, when he was coaching at Wake Forest, was somewhat handicapped in that Wake Forest had what you'd call a modest campus. His major competitors for the top athletes were Duke, which has one of the most beautiful campuses in the land, along with North Carolina and North Carolina State. And all four of these fine schools are sort of clustered together. Now, I know that when Johnny Pont first became the coach at Indiana he tried to keep prospects away from the football stadium. They had a new one in the making but the old one was drab, so Johnny would take these kids everywhere on campus except through the athletic facilities.

Peahead had the same trouble, but he was more inventive than Pont. Johnny merely avoided the issue. Peahead was cunning. He'd meet his top prospects right at the Raleigh-Durham Airport and whisk them right over to Duke's campus. The prospects wouldn't learn until they came down for good in late August or early September that they were seeing the Wake Forest campus for the first time. You have to give ol' Peahead credit, the system worked for him because he came up with some fine talent.

Paul (Bear) Bryant is no slouch when it comes to using a bit of mild trickery. Bear's a mighty good friend of mine so I know he won't mind my telling this story.

We were working hard on a prospect from East Chicago, Indiana. His name was Gene Donaldson and he was an all-state guard at Roosevelt High School. We had Gene up to East Lansing, and we figured if we lost him to any other school, it'd be Notre Dame. After all, Gene came from a very fine Catholic background. To our surprise, he wound up at Kentucky where Bear was coaching at the time. We learned later that Bear had a priest go up and spend an entire week with the Donaldson family in East Chicago. The priest convinced the family that should Gene come to Lexington, this priest would personally look after his spiritual needs and would be his friend, counselor, and confidant.

Offering a young prospect room, board, books, and tuition was pretty nice, we thought—but his own personal priest? My God, there was no way we could compete with that!

We learned later the "priest" actually was one of Bear's recruiters, disguised as a man of the cloth. I don't know what all of this did for Gene Donaldson's spiritual welfare, but he became one helluva football player and won all-America honors.

Everyone knows that recruiting is the name of the game and that you can't make chicken salad out of chicken droppings, just as you cannot compete successfully in big-time football without the blue-chip athletes. All the trick plays and well-thought-out game plans aren't worth a hoot unless you have the talent with which to execute. And Bear Bryant has been tremendously successful, proof that the man not only is a great recruiter but a great coach as well.

Recruiting was a lot easier back when schools in the North had the corner on black athletes. For a long time, the major southern schools simply didn't recruit the good black athletes. Coaches like Bryant would frequently let me know about an outstanding player of that type, and I'm proud to say that Michigan State was a forerunner not only in accepting but aggressively recruiting outstanding black scholar-athletes. Once the doors in the South were opened, though, it made things a lot more difficult.

Along with Bud Wilkinson and Darrell Royal and Bob Devaney and Bill Yeoman and John McKay, the Bear long has been one of my warmest friends in coaching. I suppose it's natural to form great friendships with other coaches because we understand the agonies and the ecstasies of our profession—much like one sewer worker would understand how much filth another sewer rat has to wade through to fix a leaky pipe. Years ago, coaching was a lot less strenuous. It was pretty much confined to the school year. There wasn't nearly as much late-night work, not so many banquets, not so many film screenings and scouting reports. Today, it's hard even to find the time for a brief vacation with the family.

But a few years back I did manage to get in a couple of days fishing with Bear Bryant at his favorite lake in Alabama. We had been out in the boat about an hour or so, with modest luck, and we soon got around to talking football instead of fishing. Bear had just come off a season in which his Crimson Tide went undefeated, won the conference title, a bowl game, and the mythical national championship. He was easily the most admired and respected man in Alabama and could have had anything he wanted.

"You know, Duffy," he drawled, "there are some folks down here in Alabama who actually believe I can walk on water."

I didn't know what kind of a comment was called for, but I allowed as how that was perfectly natural in view of his great achievements. But I was a bit surprised when ol' Bear decided to try it. He said he'd always wanted to, and he put down his fishing pole and stood up in one end of the boat and took one step out into the lake. I wasn't really

Whether back in Barnesboro with the "Alley Eleven" or coaching at Michigan State, Duffy managed to come up with the baggy-pants look. The Big Ten Sky Writers always looked forward to their visit with Duffy because they got stories and new jokes.

This was a happy time when Biggie Munn turned over the head coaching job to his long-time assistant. Things weren't always this happy between the two men, though.

Here's Duffy (far right) as an assistant coach at State with one of the tough lines he turned out. And there are those baggy pants again. Didn't they once belong to Charlie Chaplin?

When he was a junior at Syracuse, Duffy sustained a broken neck—then played one more game before sitting one out. He returned to captain the Orangemen as a senior.

When Duffy Daugherty finally began his college studies at
Syracuse he had a considerable edge on the other players.
He was four years older than the other players and working
in the coal fields of Pennsylvania had toughened him up.

The uniforms didn't always fit and the socks didn't always match, but the
game was always fun when Duffy played on the "Alley Eleven" as a
youngster in Pennsylvania. That's Duffy, third from the left, second row.

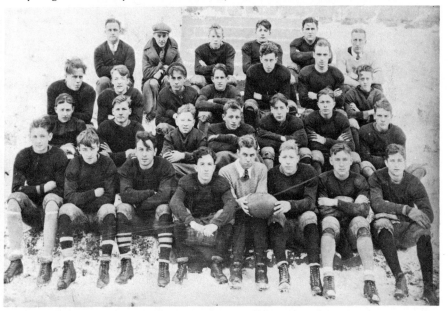

Duffy had a pool table installed in the basement of his home in East Lansing, Michigan, because he wanted his children to have the same start in life he had. Here, he lines up a shot while the late Bill Reed, then the commissioner of the Big Ten, waits his turn.

"I always told the writers and broadcasters a lot of stories when they came to our campus. I always watched closely to see which ones laughed. Those who didn't laugh didn't get invited back."

Someone once said, "Never look back because someone might be gaining on you." But when Duffy Daugherty looks back, most of what he sees is nice and good.

Running the game from the sidelines—one of the most challenging parts of coaching. This is where you watch your game plan work, or where you toss it away and start all over with "Plan X."

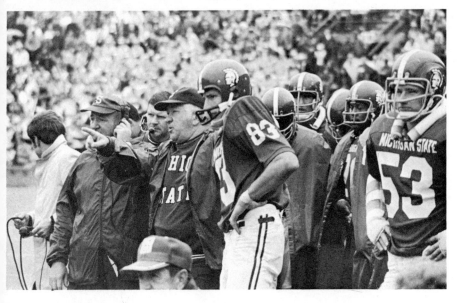

No wonder coaches get gray hairs, ulcers, and fired. Players get four-year scholarships. Coaches generally get one-year contracts.

"The thing I regret most about not coaching is the association with the great young men who play the game."

The Irish are noted for their humor and congeniality. But once in a while, a bit of Irish temper leaked through.

On days like these, the alumni never griped, the post-game questions were easy, and dinner always tasted better.

A speaker's rostrum has been almost a second home to Duffy Daugherty. He's hilarious as an after-dinner speaker, and the only time he doesn't smile is when they don't laugh at his jokes.

"Practice isn't supposed to be fun. Anybody who says getting creamed is fun should be put in a rubber room. Winning is fun."

shocked when Bear went under so I was able to compose
myself long enough to jump in and help pull him out. After
a considerable struggle we got ourselves back into the boat,
and after a bit of coughing and sputtering, Bear looked at
me with a sheepish grin and said:

"Duffy, you've gotta give me your solemn promise that
you'll never tell any of these good folks down here in
Alabama that I actually tried to walk on water."

I told him I wouldn't breathe a word of it, provided he
never tell folks up North that I helped pull him out.

Bear Bryant has turned out many, many fine football
teams, but like every other successful coach, he recruits
mainly players of what you'd call average talent. There are
very few blue-chip athletes.

If you have a great team, you'll have maybe six or seven
super athletes on your sixty-man roster. You'll have about
thirty-five to forty average athletes. But the six or seven
with exceptional skills are the ones who'll make the
difference in your season. You can't win without the
average athletes, because they're the ones who do the
workman's job and get little credit for it, simply because
they don't stand out. The gifted athletes are the ones
subjected to tremendous pressures. There were times over
the years when I worked extremely hard at recruiting a
so-called blue-chip prospect only to learn that the boy was
not blessed with extraordinary ability. You have to rely on
the judgment of your assistant coaches, and when you can
take only some thirty players a year, your judgment had
better be sound. If you're wrong on half of them, and
injuries take the normal toll, you can be in some deep
trouble.

Coaches are looking more and more to films for

guidance, but films can be misleading, too. Films will not tell you if a player is a great athlete. They might show you if he's not good, though. You might be looking at an offensive guard and if he's matched up against a very good defensive player, they might have a standoff and neither would look very good. But you might spend your time looking at a player who's up against an inferior opponent and your prospect might look like a world beater when really he has only ordinary skills.

A successful program requires a good scouting system. We used to have a group of high school coaches around the state and we'd meet with them regularly to evaluate players. I always wanted to know every good player their teams played against. This way, we got cross references and were able to pinpoint the top players in the various leagues. But you have to understand that any coach will sell his own player with a little more enthusiasm. The vast majority of your players at major universities are players who were not blessed with that great ability, but rather players who through dedication and a willingness to learn have made the progression from cannon fodder to first stringer. The average athlete is the one who takes up your coaching time. The gifted one doesn't require a lot of coaching. Mainly you have to convince him to channel that great ability, use it properly and apply proper techniques.

Over a nineteen-year career I've been fortunate to be associated with countless numbers of truly gifted athletes. But probably I remember Dean Look more than any other young man I coached. Dean was very unselfish, almost like a son to me. Before his senior year, I asked him if, for the good of the team, he'd switch from halfback to quarterback. He'd never before played that position, but Dean didn't hesitate. I knew he'd do it willingly, and successfully. That spring, he had turned down a $50,000 baseball bonus, and he went on to make the *Look* magazine All-America team.

I had two recruiting pitches. If I talked with a young man from the state of Michigan, I'd use the "state pride" approach. If I tried to sell an out-of-state prospect, I'd tell him this nation was made great by men who had the courage to tear up old roots and put down new ones in lands of greater opportunity.

We assigned members of our staff to certain geographic areas for recruiting. But a good coach never asks one of his men to do something he wouldn't do himself, so I always saved the Hawaii territory for myself. One of the best-known players we got from the Islands was a barefoot kicker named Dick Kenney. We landed Dick because he was the nephew of a good friend, Tommy Kaulukukui. And Dick kicked the football straight on with his toes extended, and I used to cringe every time he did it.

We lost five games in 1964, but I had great hopes for the '65 team. We had good talent returning, and our players were eager to wipe out the bad memories of the previous season. I felt we needed a lot of work on our kicking game, so when the players reported in the early fall for the two-a-day workouts, I told them that more games are lost through the kicking game than in any other single aspect of football. The kicking game, I stressed, is critical. So we devoted every minute of every morning workout to some phase of the kicking game—field goals, fake field goals, extra points, kick returns, kick coverage, onside kicks; you name it and we emphasized it. I don't think that in my nineteen years we ever came down harder on one subject.

On the Thursday evening before every game, we held an intimate meeting involving players and coaches, after we had dinner together. Our talks were brief and we'd point out the importance of the upcoming game and what it took to win it. On the Thursday night before our opening game, I naturally wanted to find out if the lecturing had sunk in and if all the work on the kicking game had any impact. So I pointed to a young sophomore lineman and asked, "Norm, where are most football games lost?"

"Right here at Michigan State, coach," he shot back.

Even if Norm didn't fathom what we were trying to do, the rest of the squad did. That year, Dick Kenney kicked eleven field goals including two against Michigan. One incident in the Michigan game really sticks out in my mind. Early in the contest we had a fourth down at their 30, and I sent Kenney in to try a field goal. I'm not saying we had a poor snap from center, but our holder Steve Juday couldn't reach the ball. Kenney finally picked it up and began racing all over the field—not necessarily toward the Michigan goal. I was worried on two counts—first, that he'd run the ball deep in our own territory, and then that he'd get his toes hurt. I was relieved when he finally was run out of bounds at our 45-yard line with his toes intact.

I was too busy conducting the game to give Dick constructive criticism when he returned to the bench, but after we had won the ball game I counseled him in the locker room:

"Dick, if a thing like that happens again, don't try to run with the ball. Just drop-kick the thing. I've seen you drop-kick the ball and who knows, you might make the field goal anyway. Even if you just get it into their end zone, it's a touchback and it comes out to their 20. Just don't run the ball."

Dick told me he'd never thought of it that way, but he'd certainly remember my advice. Since he was in such a receptive mood, I decided to tell him about the time such a thing happened to me:

"Our team back in Barnesboro was playing arch rival Spangler on Thanksgiving Day we had a fourth down at the Spangler 8-yard line when the coach told me to try a field goal. Well, the snap was bad and I managed to find the handle on the ball and drop-kicked it over the crossbar. It still stands out as one of my greatest thrills in football. It didn't even matter that we lost the game 69 to 3."

You always remember the good times, the good games and the good players who played for you. But coaches also remember the great athletes who got away. I'll never forget how we failed to get Tom Schoen. Now, here was a truly gifted athlete and to this day I wonder if a story I told at a high school banquet in Cleveland wasn't responsible for Tom's decision to go to Notre Dame.

John McVay, one of our assistant coaches, was at the same banquet, trying also to recruit Schoen. John had already met Schoen's father, but probably through an oversight neglected to tell me that Mr. Schoen had a slight speech impediment.

Well, one of my favorite stories is about a drawbridge attendant, Oley Olsen, who wanted to run for county supervisor. Oley didn't have any money so he got some of his friends to go out and campaign for him. They did some house-to-house canvassing, and in that neck of the woods most of the men were farmers. Oley's job was to raise the drawbridge when a tugboat was approaching, and the boats would signal him by tooting their horns. One of Oley's campaign workers called on an old farmer who had about three hundred head of cattle and asked if he'd consider voting for Oley Olsen for county supervisor.

Now, when I tell this story at banquets, I always describe the farmer as having a speech impairment, and I pretend that I have one in order to make the joke more effective.

The old farmer snorted, "I wouldn't vote for that sonofabitch for dogcatcher," and the canvasser, taken aback by the farmer's sudden show of temper, wanted to know why, so the farmer related this sad tale.

"Well sir, I'll tell you. I've been farming for twenty-five years and I never had me a good bull. Well, I had three hundred head of dairy cattle, so I went out and spent seventy-five hundred dollars for the best bull in Charlevoix County. Everything's goin' great until one day the bull becomes constipated. This went on for about ten days and I got so worried I went to see Doc Jones, the old veterinarian from Michigan State. He told me not to worry and gave me some powder and told me to mix it in a ten-gallon pail, take a funnel and insert it in the bull and give him an enema. I had everything but a funnel, but down in the shed I spotted my son's bugle. So I used the bugle for a funnel and put it in the bull's hind end and gave him a dandy enema. I got about halfway through and all of a sudden the three o'clock train went by the farm and gave out a big toot. This scared hell out of the bull, he broke his halter and started down the road with that bugle in his ass goin' like gangbusters. He was snortin' and tootin' and rantin' and fartin' and that stupid Oley raised the drawbridge and my seventy-five-hundred-dollar bull goes right smack-dab into the middle of that damned lake and drowns. Now, any sonofabitch who doesn't know the difference between a tugboat tootin' and a bull with a bugle up his ass would make a lousy county supervisor."

The story brought down the house. After the banquet, John McVay said to me, "Duff, say hello to Mr. Schoen . . ."

I'll be damned if Mr. Schoen didn't sound just like that old farmer. Naturally, I thought he was putting me on. He even told me he enjoyed the story, so I continued my conversation with him, all the time pretending to have the impediment. It seemed real funny at the time, except that Mr. Schoen really did talk like the farmer.

His son went to Notre Dame. He had an outstanding career, too. So at least our scouting report on him was good.

Polls and Other Passions

The Michigan State Spartans finished among the top ten college teams in the country seven times in my nineteen years as head coach. We won two Big Ten titles and finished second four other times. We developed thirty-three major first-string All-American players. For some of our alumni, all that seemed to be a pretty lousy batting average. But as I point out in another chapter of this book, perhaps I spoiled them, and brought on some of my own difficulties by being too optimistic.

I always said the alumni and the news media got carried away with my enthusiasm. I always thought we'd be the greatest. Matter of fact, after we won only three games in 1967, I told audiences, "We won three, lost none and were upset in seven."

Some coaches will try and tell you that the wire service polls (there are two of 'em—Associated Press, selected by the broadcasters and writers; and United Press International, picked by a panel of coaches) aren't important. Mostly, they try to talk like that in September and October, but every one of them wants to be No. 1 late in November.

Polls are important, but there is no way to select the top

team in the nation through voting, no matter who does it. Elsewhere, I'll discuss how it can and should be done. But polls, even the way they're presently conducted, are a healthy thing for college football even though there's always controversy over the rankings. Polls create interest in the game and get people talking about the ratings and the various teams around the country. Players, too, are interested in the ratings. Some coaches who put down the polls are the same ones who'll try to pour it on a lesser opponent in order to move up a notch in the ratings. For some teams without a conference affiliation and with no post-season bowl game to shoot for, being highly ranked is the only real incentive they have.

Despite some inadequacies, I've never made any secret of the fact that polls are generally healthy for the game of football. At the same time, I think the game could have used a lot more merchandising than it got in recent years. A man I respect very much is Don Canham, the athletic director at the University of Michigan, and it's his claim that college football actually lost a whole generation of fans to the pro game because of our failure to promote and merchandise our game. What Don has to say on this has a great deal of merit.

Too many people in the colleges and universities turned up their noses at the professionals and tried to pretend they didn't exist. They closed their stadia to the pros, acting as though a pro game in a college stadium or field house would somehow taint the campus. People who think that way were born for the seventeenth century and lack the vision necessary to keep the college game modern and vital.

Let's face one important fact: There's a serious economic problem today in college athletics, and a stadium sitting empty is producing no money. Whether we like it or not, colleges are the farm system and the breeding ground for the pros in many, many sports, and we might as well be brutally candid about that. The colleges and pros need each other, and even though there will forever be basic differences, they cannot be forever at each other's throats. The colleges have a perfect right to complain about some of the abuses the pros have brought about, but in the end they must live together—if not in harmony at least in a state of peaceful coexistence.

It's impossible for me to hate the pros. After all, our 1965 squad produced seven consensus All-Americans, and we've consistently contributed mightily to the pro ranks. The pros will always be with us, and so will polls. My wish always was to be ranked No. 2 at the start of the season, then on the final Saturday knock off the team ranked on top. There's a ton of pressure involved with the ratings, and sometimes it seems to be almost too much. But pressure is the name of the game. A young man feels pressure throughout his competitive life. He feels it when he's on a high school team, he's pressured when it comes to selecting a college, then there's more pressure to make the team and to excel not only on the field but in the classroom. His coach feels pressure to win, and the entire squad feels pressure because of conference standings, traditional rivalries, ratings, and a zillion other things. Despite all that, there's not another activity in a young life that better prepares a person for the greater hurdles he must overcome in later life. It's sad to see what happens to people who never experience pressure when they're growing up, because too often when they reach a critical stage in life they just don't know how to react and they're overcome by pressure instead of reacting to it and conquering their fears.

Generally, a young man who started out by making all-city or all-league or all-state is the same young man who stars in college, who makes All-American teams and becomes a star in the pros or in business. This is what life's all about! In every endeavor, the weak are separated from the strong, and those who achieve excellence dominate those who don't. Once in a while you'll find someone who can't handle getting those accolades.

At Michigan State we used to host an all-state football banquet on campus. It really wasn't a good recruiting gimmick because you didn't get a chance to spend much time with the high school seniors. But at least they got a taste of the campus and became aware of our interest in them. It was my custom to go up and down the line, shaking hands with each of the honorees. When I shook hands with this big lineman I congratulated him on being selected to the all-state team, but he curled up his lip and snarled at me, "You don't have to be nice to me, coach. I've already decided I'm going to Michigan."

I probably shouldn't have been so testy, but I snapped right back at him and said, "That's right where you belong, and I'll tell you one thing more . . . you'll never play on a football team that beats Michigan State."

He didn't, either.

One of the things we used to tell prospects was that by coming to Michigan State and playing well, they'd get more national recognition. We were proud of our tough schedule, and Dr. Hannah liked tough schedules, victories, and national recognition. He said publicly more than once that he'd schedule a team of eleven gorillas if it'd help

MSU get recognition. We did produce a lot of All-
American players—and I confess to working hard to get
that recognition for them. Ninety-nine per cent of the time I
didn't regret it, but there was an instance or two when we
produced an All-American and a sort of a monster at the
same time, the young man becoming swallowed up in his
own importance.

I always recognized the value of getting the proper
publicity. It helped lots of people, it helped the school, and
I can't think of anything or anyone it really hurt. I was
lucky at Michigan State in that we had an aggressive and
industrious sports information program. Fred Stabley has
run it for years and he has excellent assistance from Nick
Vista. Fred and Nick have always been well-liked by people
in the news media, and don't think that isn't important,
too. We always made members of the press feel welcome at
Michigan State. I realized that Fred's job was to project his
coaches and the team, so I made myself available. I'm sure I
was one of the first coaches to realize the importance of a
good public relations program.

We had more players participating in post-season all-star
games than any team in the country, and I'm sure in recent
seasons we've had as many drafted by the pros as anyone
else. Now, I know some of my critics would argue that if
we had that much talent available, there was no reason for
ever losing. All this ties in with promotion and publicity. I
admit that I worked hard at promoting and publicizing our
athletes, and so did our publicity people—because we feel
these fine young men deserve recognition. There are
coaches who don't work that hard at that part of the job.
As a consequence, their athletes do not get as much
recognition. When *they* win, the critics say the coach does

great work with mediocre talent. That's a lot of hogwash! You win with talented athletes, and because a coach develops a relationship with these young men and gets the very maximum effort out of them on the greatest number of Saturdays.

It used to be said by some nitwits, when Bump Elliott was coaching at Michigan and I was up the road at Michigan State, that "Bump's a great coach. Too bad he can't recruit. Duffy's a great recruiter. Pity he can't coach."

You simply can't separate the two, because coaching and recruiting boil down to about the same thing. That kind of criticism always got under my skin a little bit and I let it show from time to time. Maybe I shouldn't even answer it, but I coached in eleven all-star games and came out on the winning side the great majority of the time. We still hold the record for yards gained in the East-West Shrine game. I've never doubted for a minute that I had the capacity to get the most out of men.

Still, I don't think many coaches feel they're responsible for victory. Sometimes you kick yourself when something you tried backfired, and that bit of strategy may have turned an apparent victory into defeat. And it's true, I think, that coaches replay defeats much more often than victories.

When it became known I was quitting, members of the news media asked me to name my ten most memorable games. The games I listed were all defeats, like the Rose Bowl game we lost 14–12, the Iowa game we lost on that freaky fumble, like the game we lost to Purdue, the one that cost us the national championship, the game we lost to Illinois when we were No. 1 in the land, and the game we lost to Minnesota when we were favored by half a dozen touchdowns. I'll touch on those memorable afternoons later on, but the defeats do stick out in my mind.

When I selected those games, some people thought I was being negative. That wasn't it at all. I was asked for my most memorable games, not the most gratifying ones. There are several Rose Bowl trips we could have taken if just one play had been turned around. For example, in 1959 we were tied with Wisconsin, but our Spartans played one less game. The Badgers were in Minnesota playing a nationally televised game, the final game of the season. We were in Miami, Florida, to play a night game against the Hurricanes, so we watched the Minnesota-Wisconsin game on the tube before going out to the Orange Bowl. If Minnesota can beat or tie Wisconsin, we go West. Sandy Stephens was the quarterback for the Gophers, Ron Vander Kelen was the quarterback for Wisconsin. Minnesota led 7–0 in the third quarter and had the ball first and goal to go inside the Wisconsin 10-yard line. Stephens tossed a little dinky pass out in the flat, Wisconsin intercepted and ran the ball back for a touchdown and tied the game.

In the fourth quarter, Minnesota was down there knocking again and I was ready to pack for Pasadena. Same play, same result—Wisconsin intercepted and ran it back inside Minnesota territory and wound up kicking a field goal that won the game 10–7 (and talk about psychological letdowns, we went out and promptly got whipped by Miami 18–13).

In 1960, one fumble against Iowa cost us the game. In 1961, a blocked extra point cost us a trip to the Rose Bowl when all we needed to do was tie Purdue. We lost a game to Indiana 24–22, and I remember it more than any we won against the Hoosiers. We were near their goal line in the fourth quarter, and on fourth and one I disdained the field goal and went for the first down. We didn't make it, but fortunately we got another chance. In the final sixty seconds we had driven eighty yards and had a first and goal at the Indiana one. Don't you know we fumbled the snap from center, lost the ball and the ball game? The Hoosiers ran out the clock and I wanted to run under a stump.

The following Monday I went to get a haircut early in the morning before going to a staff meeting. My favorite barber worked in a hotel shop where there were six or seven chairs. I was sitting with my back to the rest of the shop and no one recognized me. Naturally, everybody was talking about the game and this was some of the conversation:

"That stupid bastard Daugherty! It doesn't take much brains to figure out that a field goal would have won the game."

"What's the matter with that idiot? Can't he add?"

"A field goal was the only logical thing to do. There's no way Indiana could have come back and scored. Hell, he's been bragging about his field goal kicker all season, and when he has a chance to win with him, the dummy blows it."

"If he insists on running, why the quarterback sneak? Doesn't that clown realize he's taking one helluva chance on a fumble?"

My barber was loving every minute of it and I was dying. Finally my barber asked all the second-guessers, "When did you guys figure out what Duffy should have done?"

One expert said the idea came to him as he was having a couple of beers on Saturday night. Another guy said he figured out watching television on Sunday how much smarter the pro coaches are. Right then I spun the damned chair around and faced a barber shop full of red faces. "Fellows," I said, "I realized what I should have done even before I got back to the locker room on Saturday afternoon. What took you so long?"

Sometimes, having to face the hometown fans was the toughest part of my whole career. I could never win enough to please them, because even a single defeat was too much. Listening to their gripes (and hearing the vicious criticism second-handed) got to be a heavy cross that I tired of carrying. In a lean year, and we didn't have many of them, going on the road was almost like an escape. Even at that you couldn't always avoid the criticism.

We always had tough games against Purdue. We played the Boilermakers nineteen times and only on eight occasions was the margin more than ten points. It was one of those unpredictable rivalries where records meant absolutely nothing. We broke streaks and prevented championships and bowl trips for each other with sickening frequency. On one occasion down at their stadium we had a ton of trouble holding onto the ball. We must have fumbled six or seven times in the first half alone, and wound up losing the game with about a dozen turnovers. We had taken our band with us. We always had a very fine band at MSU and our bandsmen performed well even in defeat with the old "show must go on" spirit.

Just as we were trudging off the field, dog tired and disheartened, the band was high-stepping around and our drum major had a custom of tossing his baton over the crossbar of the goal posts and catching it on the other side as he strutted under the bar. Wouldn't you know it? This time he blew it. He threw the thing about 75 feet in the air, then couldn't find the handle on it when it came down and it bounced crazily all over the end zone. Just then some wise guy up in the stands bellowed out, "For Christ's sake, is Duffy coaching the band, too?"

Certainly our toughest defeat against Purdue was in 1957. The defeat cost us the national championship. For the three seasons winding up in 1957, our record was 24–4. As I have said, I'm interested in polls, and in anything else that adds interest and appeal for the game of football. I don't think one poll is more valid than the other.

But perhaps the most ludicrous poll is the pre-season thing. Sometimes those pre-season ratings are a total farce. They're based on the number of veterans you have coming back from the previous season. So what if you do have twenty-three lettermen back? Maybe they're coming back from a mediocre team, and it's quite possible they're not quality football players. All that means, then, is that everyone is gonna have to endure another season of tedium and mediocrity.

The only time I really got steamed up over the polls was in 1966. That was the year of our famous, or infamous 10–10 tie with Notre Dame. I'm not saying we should have been ranked higher than Notre Dame, but surely no lower. We dominated that game in every department and to this day I don't understand why AP rated Notre Dame No. 1. The Irish went out and walloped Southern California badly at the tail end of the year, so perhaps that influenced some voters. That was a strange year from start to finish. We had been ranked on top and Notre Dame was second, but we got kicked off the No. 1 perch because we beat Ohio State by just three points, 11–8. What the voters obviously didn't take into consideration was that our game at Columbus, Ohio, was contested in such a downpour that it was impossible to see across the field. We totally dominated the game. For example, we had the ball forty-seven plays in the first half to only eighteen for the Buckeyes. Our center hiked the ball forty-two yards out of the end zone to give Ohio State a safety—but we fought back against terrible conditions in the fourth quarter and drove eighty yards for the winning touchdown. Meanwhile, Notre Dame was knocking off some powerhouse like North Carolina and got moved into the No. 1 spot. The Irish had a tough time against Purdue, but the week after our Ohio State victory we manhandled Purdue. We were leading 28–0 and could have made it 60–0, but we used our reserves throughout the second half and wound up winning 41–20.

I never believed in running up the score just to impress some pollsters. Now, you cannot tell kids not to score, and I admit that sometimes it's hard to hold down the score because it's been known to happen that a badly beaten team will just crawl up and die on you. What you can do, though, is use all your players. And even though they might be far superior to a downtrodden and discouraged team that is far behind at the time, a coach can limit his team's offense. Just eliminating the forward pass is a big step toward controlling the game. What you're really doing, in addition to controlling the score, is showing good sportsmanship and common decency.

Our great 1965 team surely must rank as one of the greatest ever to play the game. We held three teams—Notre Dame, Ohio State, and Michigan—to minus yardage on the ground. Northwestern gained only seven yards on the ground, Iowa only one yard. We had no patsies on our schedule. Our non-conference games were against Penn State, UCLA, and Notre Dame. We beat everyone in sight

—but our average margin of victory was only 19 points.

That was the first year we went to a ten-game regular season schedule. After our final game, with our record 10–0, a newsman asked if this had been my finest season. I think my answer may have stunned him.

"Well, I'd have to say it's one of the best starts we've had in recent years."

Let's get on with those "most memorable" games—and remember what I said, these aren't the most satisfying games, or the most rewarding ones. Had I been asked about those, I could not have limited the list to ten. Coaches are their own severest critics, no matter what we say about alumni and downtown coaches' groups, and we punish ourselves thinking about one call or one play that would have turned a game and perhaps an entire season all the way around.

Let's do it the way they happened, starting with our 20–13 loss at Illinois in 1956. We went into the game undefeated and ranked No. 1. We had beaten Stanford, Michigan, Indiana, and Notre Dame. We went up against the Illini without our two regular ends, Dave Kaiser and Bob Jewett. We lost Pat Burke in the Notre Dame game, and Walt Kowalczyk had been hurt at the start of the season. Still, we got in front of Illinois 13–0. Then, our best runner Clarence Peaks stepped into a hole, tore a cartilage and was out for the rest of the season. Illinois came on to score three touchdowns in the second half, all of them by Abe Woodson. He went two yards for a score in the third quarter, then got loose on scoring runs of seventy and eighty-two yards to beat us. There's no question in my mind, that loss cost us the national championship.

In 1957, we opened up with consecutive victories over Indiana, California, and Michigan and had yielded just one touchdown in twelve quarters while rolling up 108 points. Once more we were ranked tops in the country.

We were in front of Purdue 7–0 and scored what appeared to be a second touchdown. But an official disallowed the touchdown and Purdue came back to get a 7–7 tie and later win the game 20 to 13. At the half we were informed by the official that he had erred: It was a dead ball foul, the touchdown should have been allowed and the penalty assessed on the following kickoff. This was small consolation, but because of the honesty of the official in admitting the mistake, I never even mentioned the incident to newsmen following the game. We were 8–1 that season, and I'm persuaded that call cost us the Big Ten championship and the national title.

In 1960, we opened with a 7–7 tie against Pittsburgh then downed Michigan 24 to 17 before entertaining Iowa. This was a most disheartening afternoon. The Hawkeyes took a quick 14–0 lead, then we battled back with two long drives, made a two-point conversion and took a 15–14 advantage. We had possession on Iowa's 31-yard line with less than three minutes to play. It was third and two. Iowa had not made a first down in the entire second half, and it seemed as though we could have given the Hawkeyes the ball and dared 'em to score. Then came one of those freak plays that'll happen once in a lifetime. The ball popped out of one of our back's arms and went ten feet into the air. Iowa's Joe Williams picked it off and ran sixty-seven yards to score. A minute later Iowa intercepted a desperation pass, scored again, and beat us 27–15.

We had another super start in 1961. We won our first

five, giving up only 10 points altogether to Wisconsin, Stanford, Michigan, Notre Dame, and Indiana. Then we went to Minnesota to play the Gophers—made three drives of more than seventy-five yards yet could not score. We managed to stop ourselves inside Minnesota's 20 time after time, got licked 13–0, and got knocked out of the No. 1 rating and the trip to the Rose Bowl.

We touched earlier on the Illinois game of 1963—the game postponed after the tragic death of President Kennedy. We went into the game with a record of seven victories and a tie against Michigan, and we had already determined on that Saturday that we would dedicate our game to the memory of our late President. Then came the postponement, and a team that had been so ready to play couldn't get itself untracked long enough to do anything right. We had four interceptions and three fumbles and lost the game 13–0. I'll always believe that political pressure was applied by the then governor of Michigan, George Romney, to have the game delayed, because I had been informed earlier by president Hannah that the presidents of both universities had agreed to go on with the game.

The longest day in my coaching career was January 1, 1966. We had won ten in a row. We held Ohio State, Michigan, and Notre Dame to minus yardage on the ground. Our first victim during the regular season was UCLA and the 13–3 victory margin wasn't indicative of our superiority. Our fine athletes were so dedicated, so well-conditioned, that we outscored our opponents 115 to 7 in the fourth quarter of our games.

That team could have gone down as one of the all-time great aggregations in the history of the college game. Then we came to the Rose Bowl a three-touchdown favorite in a rematch against UCLA. Obviously all our players believed that. We really thought we were the "jolly green giants," but we played like mice for three quarters. We had five turnovers. Believing all that junk said and written about us was fatal. We weren't emotionally ready for the game and I knew it, but there wasn't a thing I could do about it. It was an absolutely helpless feeling.

UCLA scored twice in the second period. We had had a sophomore fielding punts in our last regular season game against Notre Dame and he fumbled a couple, so I decided to use a senior who had done the job for us a couple of years before. We had one cardinal rule about fielding punts and it was that our man was supposed to dig his heels into the 10-yard line and never back up to field a punt. Don't you know that this young man backed up to the four, tried to catch the ball, fumbled it, UCLA recovered and went in to score. I then gathered the squad around me and told them I thought UCLA would try an onside kick to their left and our right. I told our men to be prepared for it. Well, they weren't. The onside kick came, we stood around, and UCLA recovered the ball again and promptly went in for another touchdown. We played like the dickens in the fourth period and scored twice, but missed both attempts for 2-point conversions.

After the game I was totally down. I went back to my hotel suite and all I wanted was to be left alone. Later on that evening I did take a call from Jack Curtice, who then was up at the University of California at Santa Barbara.

Since Jack was an old and trusted friend around whom we could be comfortable, Francie and I decided to spend a few days with him. Anyway, he promised me he and I would team up on the golf course against a couple of old retired Army colonels. They beat us, too—using wooden shafts!

No sooner had I settled down at Santa Barbara but I came down with an attack of that rare California virus and the doctors decided, as a precautionary move, to put me in the hospital for a day or two. Just to show you the type of loyalty we have at Michigan State, right from the custodians on up to the top administrators, I was in the hospital only a few hours when I received a telegram from the ruling board of trustees at Michigan State University, stating that "We wish you a speedy recovery, by a vote of four to three."

Perhaps the most talked about tie in football history is the Michigan State-Notre Dame 10–10 deadlock of 1966. We went into the game with a 9–0 record but ranked No. 2 because we had beaten Ohio State only 11–8 in a driving rainstorm while Notre Dame was decisively whipping North Carolina.

We felt we were the better team. We rushed more, passed more and recorded more first downs. With all credit to Notre Dame, the Irish took advantage of a fumble that led up to their field goal, and got off a long touchdown pass just before the half. We moved the ball more decisively and appeared the stronger team, defensively and offensively. But since we did not win the game, I couldn't very well come out and say we were deserving of the No. 1 honor. But to this day, I don't think Notre Dame deserved it, either.

We had a ton of disappointments in 1967 since we won only three games, but I'd have to rank our 21–17 loss to Southern California in the second game of the campaign as one of the most discouraging of my career. The Trojans went on to become No. 1 in the country, and we should

"If they make a movie out of my life, do you really think Rod Steiger could handle the title role?"

Andy Kerr, the one-time Colgate coach, used to scout the colleges for talent for the East-West Shrine classic. It became a haven not only for Michigan State players, but for Duffy as well, and he made certain the game was more fun than work.

"I never prepare notes when I'm gonna make a speech. I always figure I'll think of something appropriate to say. When the day comes that I can't, I guess I won't get invited anyplace."

Michigan State was No. 1 many times during Duffy's nineteen years as head coach. Being No. 1 after the final game was the best feeling of all. (Left to Right, Pat Gallinagh, George Webster, Duffy, Drake Garrett, Jerry Jones, and Jeff Richardson.)

The day was warm, the sun was out, the fans were happy, and the Spartans were winning. Those were the best days of all.

The "feud" between Duffy and Biggie Munn sometimes smouldered, sometimes flared up, but more often than not didn't even exist.

Sending in a play from the sidelines is great if the play works. When it doesn't, you always wonder why they didn't build a little hole under the bench—just in case the coach wants to crawl in it once in a while.

The look on the coach's face is a dead giveaway. Things are not going well for the Spartans. Most of the time, though, they did.

The secret to longevity in coaching is winning a whole lot more than you lose. The fellows shaking hands at midfield are two of the most prolific producers of victory in the history of football—Woody Hayes of Ohio State and Duffy Daugherty of Michigan State.

Surely Duffy's wit and story-telling abilities helped Michigan State in its recruiting of top high school athletes. But one time, a well-told story turned a young man to Notre Dame (but Duffy still tells the story).

The late Red Sanders and Duffy are looking at the same crystal ball prior to the 1956 Rose Bowl game, but getting different answers. Michigan State won the game.

Did the putt miss the cup by that much, was the bass only that long (or did we measure the fish "across"?), or did the referee miss the call by that far?

When Duffy reminisced over this picture, he said: "They must have been congratulating me over one of THEIR teams. When we didn't win quite so many, it was always MY team."

That's Duffy on the far right as Biggie Munn assembled his first coaching staff at Michigan State. Miami of Ohio is called "the cradle of coaches," but Michigan State had more than a dozen assistant coaches under Biggie, and Duffy who went on to head coaching jobs at major colleges and universities. (From left: Louis F. Zarza, Leverne Taylor, Head Coach Clarence L. "Biggie" Munn, Forest Evashevski, and Duffy.)

Those are oranges the Rose Bowl queen and her court are holding around Duffy's head, but the occasion was the 1956 Rose Bowl. Duffy kept the smile on his face even after the game because Michigan State won the game.

All-Americans always made Duffy smile and he's flanked by two of them as the Spartans arrived in Pasadena for the 1956 Rose Bowl game. The fellow on the left is quarterback Earl Morrall, who can still throw the football, while guard Buck Nystrom is on the coach's right.

have beaten them. What would have been the winning touchdown was called back on us in the final quarter. We had driven seventy-five yards and had a fourth and two on Southern Cal's 5-yard line. We faked an option and threw a pass to Al Brenner, who was all alone in the end zone. The officials called it back, saying our other end was blocking downfield, but the film clearly showed it was a bad call.

Our 25–20 loss to Ohio State at Columbus in 1968 ranks right up there, too. We went into the game with a 4–2 record and the Buckeyes were No. 1 at the time. We were trailing 25–20, and three times in the last half we marched downfield, only to lose the ball on a series of freak plays. We have no one to blame but ourselves for that loss—but when you blow a chance to knock off the No. 1 team it hurts more than ever.

The year 1972 was my last one, and it didn't get to be fun until I announced my resignation. We opened with a victory over Illinois, then got bumped by Georgia Tech, Southern Cal, and Notre Dame.

Bo Schembechler had a clearly superior Michigan team, but records never matter in that rivalry. We lost 10–0 in a game we should have won. We didn't complete a single pass and had three of them intercepted—but still we had every right to be the winner when the final gun sounded. We were penalized in the second quarter and had a touchdown taken away. Michigan should have been penalized on the Wolverines' only touchdown in the fourth quarter. It was the only time in nineteen seasons I ever got a call from the conference office telling me I was right and the officials were wrong. Try as I might, though, I never could get Bo to reverse that score and put it down as a victory for Michigan State. I'll always believe that had we gotten the victory we deserved over Michigan, we never would have been tied by Iowa—and even with all the disappointments of my final season, we still could have won the conference championship.

No matter, though, I still would have quit. That decision was a long time in the making.

They Called Me "Impish" (and a few other things)

There's an old story about the death of a prostitute and her funeral. The madam closed the house of commercial affection for the afternoon and along with several of her ladies attended the last rites. It was a simple service, lasting only about ten minutes, and near the end of the rites the minister wondered "Is there someone here today who would like to say a few words about Margie before she is taken to her final resting place?"

With that, the madam stood up and proclaimed proudly, "Margie was the finest little hooker who ever worked for me."

Then she sat down, and the young girl next to her began sobbing. "That's the trouble with this business," she cried. "You have to die before someone says something nice about you."

Maybe I've been lucky. I've had mostly nice things said about me, and my relationship with the men and women of the news media has been mainly pleasant. The late Herman Hickman said the trick to getting along with alumni was to keep them sullen but not mutinous. Maybe my secret to getting along with the press was to keep them humored. It's been said there are only two kinds of coaches—those who have been fired, and those who are going to get fired. I was one of the lucky ones. Even though folks sometimes suggested I be canned, I'm thankful I was able to walk away on my own, without being told it was all over. Thank goodness, we won a lot more than we lost or I might have taken the criticism even more seriously than I did. My first season was terrible, then we had three dandy ones before stumbling through a 3-5-1 record in 1958. When some reporters asked me during spring practice who I was most happy to see back that season, I told them without a moment's hesitation, "Me!"

The main problem with the press—and when I use that term I mean newspapermen, magazine writers, radio, and television broadcasters, everyone—is that they don't understand very much about the game they're covering. The awful truth is most of them don't know a blitzing line-backer from a naked reverse. But I always tried to understand that they had a job to do, and asked only in return that they make an attempt to understand mine. I've been everywhere from the penthouse to the outhouse in coaching, and fortunately for me I was able to figure out which members of the press, alumni, and so forth would be riding the crest of your fortunes, and which ones would let your success, or lack of it, govern what they wrote or said. You have to know who the fair-weather folks are. Quite often, a writer or broadcaster will want you to win so badly that he'll expect you to, even when you're saddled with a medi-ocre team. Then, when you don't do as well as he expected, he'll rip your guts out because of his own disappointment.

In a sense, I was my own worst enemy in this respect. I was always tremendously optimistic about the Spartans' chances. I just couldn't help myself. After all, I had recruited these fine young men and I thought always that they were the finest young men in the whole world. I'd conveniently forget that Michigan and Notre Dame and Purdue recruited just as vigorously and got the same enthusiasm out of their programs. I can never remember a season when I didn't tell the whole world that our team had a chance to be a title contender. I guess in my heart I really believed that, but I'd have said the same thing if I had been coaching at Chickamauga Tech.

I was always tempted to have a couple of big freshmen linemen undertake a special assignment, but I never got around to it. Maybe it would have taken some of the heat off me. I thought it'd be a good idea to have these big linemen hoist me up on their shoulders after each game— win or lose—and carry me off the field. Then the fans and the press would say, "Look, there goes old Duffy again. He ain't much of a coach, but those players sure love him."

I've been called many things, especially after tough losses, but I suppose the descriptions most frequently used are "genial" and "the impish Irishman" and things like that. Sometimes it was hard to smile in the face of adversity, but a smart coach never blames fine young men for defeats. I didn't blame them, either. I always liked what the late President Truman said, "If you can't stand the heat, then you'd better get out of the kitchen."

Some members of the press had a field day over the years with the so-called "Biggie-Duffy Feud." Look, Biggie Munn gave me my first coaching job. He got me started in this business. He brought me to Syracuse, then brought me to Michigan State. When he quit coaching and became athletic director, he recommended me for the head coaching job. If it hadn't been for Biggie Munn, I might still be mining coal in Pennsylvania. I even take credit for Biggie's being inducted into the Football Hall of Fame. After six years of my coaching they could appreciate his coaching greatness.

If you expect me to tell you that we never had differences of opinions—and strong ones at that—I can't do that. We've stood toe to toe, eyeball to eyeball, and yelled at each other because we are both strong-willed individualists who say what we think. But through the years, we've maintained a healthy respect for each other. We'd flare up and have our say, then the next minute be having a beer together.

When Biggie became athletic director and I became head coach, it was a difficult transition for both of us. He had been accustomed to the spotlight, and now it was my turn. Perhaps Biggie thought I wasn't appreciative enough, I don't know. But we both have pretty good-sized egos, and we had our clashes. Certain people magnified them, and there were factions that supported Biggie, and factions that supported me. I always thought that was ridiculous. Why did anyone have to be a Biggie person or a Duffy person? Everyone should have been content just to be a Michigan State person, because the school will be around a long time after the two of us and all the All-American athletes have vanished.

The worst of it happened late in the 1958 season. Remember now, we were coming off three spectacular seasons in a row, and this was only my fifth season as head coach. We went into a tailspin, losing to Purdue by 8 points, to Illinois by 16, to Wisconsin by 2, and to Indiana by 6. Then we went up to play Minnesota, Biggie's alma

mater. There had been recurring reports that Biggie
wanted to become athletic director at Minnesota, and it's
natural that he particularly wanted our team to show up
well against the Gophers. Stating it bluntly, we stunk out the
joint, losing 39–12. After the game, Biggie was quoted as
saying words to the effect that it was shameful to work
years to build a football empire, then watch it crumble
away. Some segments of the press treated the whole thing
like World War III, and to this day some folks won't let it
die.

President Hannah called the two of us in, and made it
perfectly clear that the university was more important than
anyone's ego. Both Biggie and I left his office much wiser
men. Now, I know it upset Biggie that I was able to go
directly to Dr. Hannah. But I had that understanding from
the start, and Biggie knew it, and I enjoyed the relationship
I had with Dr. Hannah. Every year, win or lose, whether we
had a great year or a not-so-good one, the two of us sat
down and reviewed everything. He simply wanted
excellence in everything, and he wasn't one of those
namby-pamby presidents who thought of athletic
competition as a necessary evil or a part of the academic
life that had to be tolerated. Like I said, when I took the
job it was agreed that when Biggie and I disagreed—and it
was inevitable that we would—I would have the right to go
directly to the president. Down through the years I never
felt I was going over Biggie's head or behind his back
because I had taken the job with that understanding.

When Biggie and I disagreed it was tough to keep the
spat a secret, and we always found people eager to capitalize
on that sort of thing. Once something like that snowballs
there's little, if anything, you can do to stop it. I can't tell

you how many times Biggie and I would have our own little summit meetings to discuss the latest rumor . . . he'd heard something I allegedly said about him, I read something he allegedly said about me. But right to the end, Biggie and I could communicate and discuss our problems. I cannot say that my lines of communication were always that open with some members of the press.

In all honesty, most reporters really don't understand the complexities of coaching. Most of them never played the game beyond the sand-lot or high school stage, if at all, and I've always felt that those who never engaged in spirited athletic competition themselves can never possibly understand the human drama of it. At ABC Sports, there's a very profound string of words at the beginning and the closing of the popular "Wide World of Sports" program, and they speak of the "thrill of victory and the agony of defeat." Just think about those two things for a minute—the THRILL of victory and the AGONY of defeat. Now, I'm not saying that victory and defeat are akin to life and death, although if you string together enough losses, you can almost feel the life ebbing out of you, and when the alumni and the athletic director and the press are jumping on you at the same time you'll wish you were dead.

I'm convinced that the thrills and the agonies of victory and defeat in competition are unique, and that it takes a special kind of person to understand them. Even though I've enjoyed a good relationship with the press over the years, I nonetheless feel that most writers and broadcasters have nothing more than a superficial knowledge of the game, and precious little understanding of the little bits and pieces of life that are woven in and out and around the young men who are the competitors on the field.

Most of the people who regularly cover a team want that team to win. They're fans as well as reporters, but they have to think of their readers and their reputations. The more competitive the press situation, the more sensational the stories. I can truthfully say that I never lied to a reporter in order to protect myself. I've done some fibbing here and there to protect a player, though. One year one of our star players was performing well below expectations and as a result the team was sub-par, too. I had several meetings with the young man and I knew he was carrying some massive personal problems around on his shoulders. To bench him, I thought, would have compounded his problems and possibly destroyed his confidence. To tell reporters about his problems would have been a violation of confidence and might have done a great deal more harm. Even some of my assistant coaches didn't know about the situation, so we rode it out together, just the player and me. Finally he got things straightened around, off the field and on. His could have been a wasted life—the problems were that gigantic. But today he's a happy and well-adjusted contributor to society and a fine family man. And I don't think I'm unique in the way the matter was handled, because most of the coaches I've known over the years are far more interested in the life of a young man than in winning a football game.

There were times, I'll admit, when I wanted to scream out at the top of my lungs and tell everything, but there just are some things that are better left unsaid. I got myself in enough hot water with my optimism, so I decided when it came to the personal lives of my players and staff, I'd try to remember the old adage that it's better to keep your mouth shut and have people think you a fool than to open it and remove all doubt.

As I think back on the good times and the bad, they were mostly good. The "downs" really were few: the recurring reports of the Biggie-Duffy feud, the report one year that our coaching staff was drinking and carousing around, the criticism that I was spending too much time running around the country at speeches and clinics instead of coaching, and the report that we had racial problems on the team. Naturally, the bad news always descended when we weren't winning as many games as some folks thought we should. I'd like to put the Biggie-Duffy feud to rest for good, but I suppose some folks will never let it die. But I have never lost my gratitude toward Biggie Munn for giving me the opportunity to coach.

Many observers never seem to understand the public relations side of coaching. If you're coaching at a big-time school with a tradition of excellence, you have to be a lot more than a mere coach. On the field you're a strategist, coach, psychologist, father, you name it. Off it, you're a public relations man for the team, your school, and your community. It ticked me off good that when we lost a few games the know-it-alls came out of the woodpile and blamed me for being away from East Lansing so much. Hell, where did they think we got those football players? The wider acceptance a coach has throughout the country, the easier it is to recruit. Hopefully, in a span of nineteen years, the name Duffy Daugherty came to mean something in places other than East Lansing, Michigan.

I always enjoyed the visits of the Big Ten Skywriters. Writers from all around the conference would visit each campus in the Big Ten early in fall practice, and we always looked forward to their visits. One year they had stopped in Columbus the day before to look in on friendly old

Woody and his Buckeyes. Woody kept twenty-four sports writers, Commissioner Bill Reed, and his assistant off the practice field—behind a locked gate—for more than an hour. When Woody finally appeared later, he explained, "I wanted to give my players hell for their mistakes, and I didn't want any outsiders to hear it. I don't believe in whipping my guys in the newspapers."

That set things up perfectly for me. When the writers arrived at our practice field next day, they found our gates locked, too. But I kept them waiting only five minutes, then explained: "I kept you guys out because I wanted to praise my players, and I didn't wanna do it in front of strangers."

Another time, when the writers came to visit, Fred Stabley and Nick Vista pried their eyes open with a batch of bloody marys then we all gathered around the outdoor pool. We were going good at the time and one of the writers wanted to know the secret of our success (thank God someone asked, or the whole gag would have been loused up).

So I went into elaborate detail, explaining that we used the most up-to-date scouting methods and advanced scientific know-how. "Frankly, gentlemen, I know it may sound immodest, but it's the way we coach here at Michigan State."

At that time, a number of student employees were working around the pool, so I summoned one rather studious-looking young man to my side. I had a football in my hand, and I asked the young man if he knew what it was. He said he did, that he'd seen one once or twice, and I told him that I was going to explain how to catch the thing. Then I rambled on with a drawn out scientific explanation of the thing, why it travels through the air like it does, how it is propelled, and so on and so forth. I briefly explained the proper way to catch it, and all the while the Skywriters are just standing around gawking. Then I instructed the young student to go to the far end of the pool. When he got there, I threw a long pass in his direction, and he nonchalantly reached up and picked it off with one hand.

"There you see it, gentlemen," I smirked, "pure, coaching genius."

The young man who caught the ball was Ernie Clark, one of the finest ends who ever played at Michigan State.

Coaches sometimes take themselves too seriously, and I've been in that group on occasion. I know I read too many sports pages and listened to too many broadcasts during the season. My pal Bud Wilkinson told me he never checked any of that stuff once the season had begun. I probably would have been better off had I followed Bud's practice. And of course the press never quite learned how to control my enthusiastic optimism. The Sky Writers invariably would pick Michigan State to finish either first or second in the conference, and I'd have been mad as hell had they picked us any lower.

One time I was making a speech in Rochester, New York, for the Kodak people and there was a lot of speculation at the time that I was all set to take the Texas A & M job. A newsman from Detroit showed up in Rochester and rode with me on the train back to Michigan. He showed me some copy he had filed for the afternoon paper, saying that "the little round man from Michigan State will leave." I told him he'd be wise to call his office when the train stopped at Buffalo and change that story. He did, and the newspaper simply changed it to say that "the little round man from Michigan State will stay."

That very next year, the same newspaper printed a pack of lies, saying our coaches were a bunch of playboys and that

Biggie and I were openly feuding. I guess I was never any madder at the media.

My first season at Michigan State as head coach, we lost three of our first four games by a total of 11 points, and a writer friend of mine from Cleveland, Jack Clowser, came to me in the locker room after our 20–19 loss to Notre Dame.

"Duff," he said, "why don't you do what Woody Hayes does at Ohio State? You know, right before he sends his Buckeyes onto the field, he personally leads them in singing the Ohio State fight song."

That's fine, I told Jack, but I don't even know Ohio State's fight song. Things got a great deal better for us, but to this day I still don't know Woody's song. I do know that when Woody sings, his players listen.

I got sick and tired of all the tired old comments coaches would make each season. They'd all say the same thing, that if they could get off to a fast start and avoid injuries, they'd be a decent team . . . that they were gonna play the games one at a time (is there any other way?) . . . that they were gonna show up on Saturday (it'd be wild if they didn't, huh?) . . . that every position on the team was open. I wanted to be different.

When I was asked if improper shoes contributed to our loss to Washington on the artificial turf at Seattle, my answer was, "Blaming the shoes for our defeat (42–16) would be like blaming the Johnstown flood on a leaky toilet in Altoona."

Maybe I figured that if I set my sights on winning the national championship, the squad perhaps would become infected with that feeling, and who knows, maybe we'd win three or four games we had no business winning?

But there's no way to keep everyone in the press happy, any more than you can keep all the alumni happy. There's a story that explains the frustration of even trying.

A little boy, an old man, and a jackass were making their way across the burning desert. All three were walking. When they passed the first village, the people muttered, "Look at those idiots walking in the hot sand. At least one of them could be riding."

So the old man boosted the little boy up onto the jackass and they went on. Soon they came to another village, and the people there were critical, too.

"Look at that inconsiderate little boy," they said, "making that poor old man walk in the burning sand."

The little boy got down and the old man rode the jackass. Soon they passed another settlement and the people cried aloud, "Boo on you, old man, for making that poor little boy walk in the sand while you ride."

So they both got atop the jackass and rode. Soon they came to an oasis and began to cross a creaky old bridge. Under the heavy weight, the bridge collapsed and old man, boy, and jackass plunged into the water below. The old man could swim and managed to save himself and the boy, but the jackass drowned. All this proves is that you can't please all the people all the time, and you'll lose your ass if you try.

Sometimes I expected far too much of our teams and our staff. There's such a thing as setting unrealistic goals. It's like Elsie the cow who was farmed out to pasture after many years of faithful service. As she settled down in this lush, green field, a big brute of a bull sidles over to the fence separating them and said, "Hi, I'm Ferdinand the bull. What's your name?"

Elsie was spoiled from the attention she'd had over the years, so she stuck her snoot in the air and swished her tail just once, then walked haughtily away. For days, she wouldn't pay any attention to the bull. The more she ignored him, the more determined he was to know her better. One day, the long period of rejection got to him. He could take it no longer. He pawed at the ground, snorted, got up a full head of steam, and leaped over the fence right into Elsie's pasture.

By golly, she was impressed! She sauntered over to where he had landed and introduced herself. "Did you say you're Ferdinand the bull?"

"Just call me Ferdinand," he replied in a weak, squeaky voice about two octaves higher than normal. "That fence was a mite higher than I thought."

Over the years, I've developed great sympathy for Ferdinand. I know the feeling.

But I can honestly say I never met a member of the press corps I didn't like. However, I have a few names on my list in the event I should ever change my mind.

A Funny Thing Happened

One of the criticisms directed at coaches is that they control the game, call all the plays, and take the game away from the young men who are playing it. You can make a convincing argument for either method—calling all the plays yourself, or letting your quarterback do it. I've used both systems, depending on the talent available and my mood at the time.

Once, in a critical game, we had the ball fourth and one at Wisconsin's 38. We were in front 20–14 with some six minutes left in the game. Question was: Do we punt and try for the coffin corner to put the Badgers in the hole, then depend on our defense to hold them off, or do we go for the first down and try to move in for a touchdown or a field goal that would put the game out of reach?

Seventy-eight thousand quarterbacks in the stands were expressing their opinions, and our quarterback looked over to where I was standing, arms folded, on the sidelines. It was obvious to everyone he wanted instructions from me. I gave him no signal at all and instead turned and walked down the sidelines with my back to him. After the game, a reporter asked me why I didn't help my quarterback.

"That kid has a four-year scholarship," I told him. "My contract is a one-year deal. Let him make his own decisions."

In 1959, Dean Look made a decision on his own and it turned out to be one of the funniest incidents of my long career in football. We were playing Notre Dame on national television. It was a sloppy game and we were tied 0–0. Both teams were fumbling back and forth, and about midway through the second quarter the Irish fumbled and we got the ball right in front of our bench.

I figured this was a good time to run our power sweep. We had two good halfbacks, Herb Adderly and Gary Ballman, with Ron Hatcher at fullback. Monte Stickles was playing left defensive end for Notre Dame, and I knew Ballman could handle him. We had the wide side of the field to the right, and I could envision the play working for a long gainer for us. We had what we used to call "student body right." We'd pull both guards and one tackle. With three men pulling, Ballman blocking Stickles, and Look handing off to Adderly—well, it just couldn't miss. So I grabbed a second stringer who had nothing to do on this play except stay out of the way of progress and told him to go into the huddle and deliver the play to Look.

He gave the message to the quarterback, and I could see Dean nodding. He'd do that on rare occasions when he agreed with one of my decisions. As the play developed, I was watching Ballman, and sure enough he put Stickles right on his fanny. Then I saw the three men who had pulled—Don Wright, Palmer Pyle, and Mickey Walker—and then came Hatcher with Adderly trailing. But Adderly didn't have the damned ball!

Instead of handing off to Herb, Dean decided to keep the thing and run a bootleg. He fooled everybody on both teams except the Notre Dame right end, who smacked him about five yards behind the line of scrimmage. Somehow Dean squirmed loose, avoided a couple of other latecomers, zig-zagged around for what seemed like an eternity and finally was knocked out of bounds on the Notre Dame 7-yard line after gaining more than forty yards.

I yanked him right out of the game. After all, you have to have discipline, and as soon as he came to the sidelines he had a wide grin across his face and I grabbed him. I was really steaming and I said, "Dean, we don't even have a play like that."

He never quit grinning and said, "Duff, you ought to. It's a dandy."

He explained that he really didn't have control of the football as he was trying to effect the hand-off, so he just kept it. The reason it worked so well is that no one but Dean Look knew what was going on, so every player was really faking by accident. Man, if we could fake with that kind of convincing authority every time, we'd score a lot more touchdowns.

In Walt Kowalczyk's sophomore year we were 7-7 against Notre Dame and we had the ball at the Irish 4. We were using the belly series and our quarterback, Earl Morrall, faked to one man then gave the ball to Walt. He had the ball in his left arm when he saw the cornerman coming at him, and he tried to switch the ball to the other arm so he could stiff-arm the tackler. In so doing he fumbled and Notre Dame fell on the ball. Fortunately, we got the ball back on a fumble a couple of plays later and went on to win the game 21-7. I didn't say anything to Walt after the game since he was a sophomore and a pretty sensitive young man, but a couple of weeks later we played Wisconsin, and it was raining as we jogged through our Friday afternoon workout at Camp Randall Stadium. I called Kowalczyk over and tried to put it to him gently:

"Walt, a couple of weeks ago you fumbled because you tried to change the ball from one hand to the other. Never do that just to use the straight-arm. That's sand-lot football. You're 210 pounds and fast, so just use your tremendous speed and power. When you get past the line of scrimmage, forget about changing hands. Just run over people. If you get five yards a crack, you'll be an All-American and you'll help Michigan State win a lot of games."

Walt nodded and assured me he understood. On our second play from scrimmage that next afternoon, Earl Morrall faked, handed the ball to Kowalczyk, and Walt burst right through the line. Sure as the devil, he changed the ball from his left arm to his right and hit the cornerman with one of the most vicious straight-arms I've ever seen. Fifteen yards farther downfield, he saw a defensive back coming at him, so darned if he didn't change hands again and knock the defensive back right on his can with another stiff-arm. Walt went seventy-two yards for the touchdown that started the Spartans on their way to a 27–0 triumph—but if he had absorbed my coaching genius, we'd have gained five yards and had the ball at our own 33.

We were fortunate in that we managed to get comfortably ahead in a number of games and one day we had a five- or six-touchdown lead. I had used everyone on the bench in an effort to hold down the score. Finally, with about thirty seconds to play, we had the ball on the other team's 11-yard line, so I told our people to run straight ahead and not call any time outs. We were using Bobby Popp at quarterback, and he normally worked with the scouting team. All of a sudden, he called a 21-reverse. That was the last thing I wanted to call and the last thing the other team expected and so it went for a touchdown. Bobby was all smiles when he came off the field, and I asked him why in the name of good sense he called that particular play.

"Well, coach, I'll tell you," he explained. "My number is 13. You had John in at wingback, and his number is 9. Since the two of us are roommates, I just took the 13 and the 9, added 'em up and figured it'd be nice to call the 21-reverse."

"Bobby," I said, "13 and 9 add up to 22, not 21."

"Coach, if I were as smart as you, we wouldn't have scored."

Bobby was one of the most popular players we ever had at MSU and the other players loved him. He had a wonderful sense of humor and contributed a great deal to the Spartans though he rarely played. Another time we were well in front in the final quarter, and I asked Bobby if he thought he could take them in from the 40. I was concerned about Bobby handling our offense, since he spent most of his time running the offense of our next opponent. Bob assured me he'd be O.K., and he was. He took us in for a score in two plays, and before he even got off the field he yelled to me, "Hey, Duff, is that fast enough for you?"

I always encouraged the players to call me Duffy or Duff, and to call the assistant coaches by their first names. I don't think it ever caused a diminishing of respect, because not one time in nineteen seasons did I ever have to discipline a player for poor conduct on the field, and I never had a single player question my decisions on the field.

One time in 1955 we opened the game with a surprise play—Morrall faking a sweep and throwing a bootleg pass.

Earl executed perfectly and dropped the football right into the arms of a very fine end, John (Big Thunder) Lewis. But big John dropped the thing. A couple of games later I called him aside and told him:

"John, we're gonna open today's game the same way we did a couple of weeks ago, except this time it's gonna work. And you know why it's gonna work? Because you're gonna catch the football. And you're gonna go for a touchdown. Now, if you don't catch it, you just keep right on running, right out through the tunnel and into the locker room and take off your uniform and don't ever come back."

I don't know to this day whether John believed me, but I know he didn't drop the ball, and he went fifty yards for a touchdown.

Everything was fun in those days. Our players not only were talented but they were funny, too. One time we were far ahead of Michigan and we were using our fifth and sixth stringers late in the game. One of our scouting team ends got ten yards behind the Michigan secondary and dropped a pass that had touchdown written all over it. When he came to the sidelines he was yelling at me, "Coach, did you hear that deafening roar, that noise, all that action?"

I told him I heard no such thing.

"C'mon, coach, it was the programs. A hundred thousand people rustling through their programs trying to find out who that idiot wearing number 97 is."

Surely one of the most remarkable players we ever had at Michigan State was Leroy Bolden, and one time he shot through the line and a defensive tackle grabbed him by the seat of the pants. But Leroy was squirming and his legs pumping so fast he ran right out of his pants and continued on down the field, wearing only his jersey and his jock strap, and he scored a touchdown. When he came to the sidelines, we got the equipment man to get him another pair of pants and we formed a circle around Leroy so he could put 'em on. I peeked into the makeshift huddle and said, "Boldy, that's the best showing you've made all season."

I never tolerated profanity because it was my feeling that if one player on the squad objected to it, he shouldn't have to be exposed to it. Occasionally we'd get a player with a habit of swearing, but we could always break it. I'd tell the players that as college students, they should have enough of a vocabulary to pick some word other than a profane one.

One of the most dedicated players we had was Dan Currie. In the spring of his freshman year, Dan was making a strong bid for a varsity job. But he'd get mad at himself when he'd miss a block or blow an assignment. He'd swear aloud, but always at himself. When all else failed, I had to resort to my toughest posture to break Dan's cursing. One day in practice after he had turned loose a torrent of swear words that would make a Marine drill instructor blush, I blew my whistle and halted practice. I told Dan that swearing was a sure sign of a limited vocabulary and had nothing to do with masculinity or toughness. I warned him that if there came one more outburst, he could pack his gear and get off the squad.

On the very next play, Currie missed the same block he'd been missing all afternoon. Every man on both sides of the line stopped cold, wondering what Dan would say. He stiffened up, bit his lip, then broke out into a possumlike grin. As he walked back to the huddle he said—almost under his breath—"Excuse me, gentlemen." Dan Currie not only improved his vocabulary but became one of the greatest players in MSU history.

It's tough to get mad at someone who swears at his own shortcomings—like the parishioner who shook the preacher's hand after the Sunday service and added, "That was a damned good sermon today."

The minister was embarrassed by the strong language and told the worshiper that while he appreciated the compliment, he felt the profanity was unnecessary.

"By God, I mean it," the parishioner repeated. "I think that was one of the best damned talks I ever heard. Matter of fact, I was so impressed I just dropped a hundred dollar bill in the collection plate."

The preacher gasped, "The hell you did!"

It was my good fortune to coach in eleven all-star games. They were always fun for me, and I tried to make them fun for the participants. After all, these outstanding seniors were being rewarded for their excellent work and they deserved a few laughs. When I first coached in the East-West Shrine Game in San Francisco, I announced right off the bat that it was going to be fun and that we'd work out just once a day. I told the players we'd work mostly in sweat clothes in the afternoons, and that they could go into town every night, stay out late and sleep in the next morning. The players loved the system, but Andy Kerr, the old Colgate coach and a grand old man, didn't agree with my philosophy at all.

Andy was the manager of our East team, but I told him nicely to withhold his criticism until after the game. Then I told the players the only thing I asked of them in return was a victory—and they gave it to me. We had an absolute ball! Since the players came from different offensive systems, we devised a simple set of signals—so simple, in fact, that even the other team could figure them out. One of them was "Hi diddle diddle, the cat and the fiddle, here comes the fullback right up the middle."

Later on, when we had our "down" years at Michigan State, I often wondered why I didn't switch over to the system that had been so successful. It was so much fun that even old Andy Kerr got into the swing of things and began having fun with the squad. Matter of fact, he told me lots of funny stories that I've used over the years.

Like most Scotsmen, Andy was frugal but had a keen sense of humor. One of his favorite stories concerned Sandy McTavish, who had taken his wife fishing off Long Beach, California. Unfortunately, the boat capsized. Sandy managed to swim to shore but his dear wife could not be found. Sandy waited around in town three or four days while the search for her body was conducted, but when it could not be found he decided to return to his job in New York State. He had been home about a week when he received a telegram from authorities in Long Beach informing him that his wife's remains had been washed ashore. They also told him that attached to her body was a rare species of fish and that the seaquarium in Long Beach had offered $25,000 for the fish. The authorities needed instructions from Sandy as to what to do about the situation.

Sandy wasn't one to waste a lot of money on wordy telegrams so he promptly wired back: "Sell fish. Reset bait."

Bobby Dodd used to tell the story of the time his team first saw the T-formation. In the first game his outfit was beaten 83–0. Then they got scalped 90–0. In the third game they got whipped 34–0 and in the fourth game they lost by a score of 10–0. Someone asked Dodd how his team managed to improve so much on defense and Dodd replied, "We

finally figured out the other team always gave the ball to
the player with the helmet."

Most coaches have senses of humor. You have to be able
to laugh. It keeps you from crying lots of times. The late
Red Sanders of UCLA had a wry sense of humor, and I
remember a time when we sat through a long and boring
speech at a coaches' convention. Everyone was sore and
totally disgusted when we finally got out of the banquet
hall, but it was Red who succinctly described the speaker's
efforts as "the oratorical equivalent of a blocked punt."

Coaches are forever complaining about officiating, and
I've done my share. Sometimes I know my criticism has
been justified, even though I never had a single defeat
turned into victory by an official's admission of error. Once
when we were all set to play Notre Dame, I was mildly
apprehensive when I noted that the referee had an Irish
name. But as the game progressed, and we were doing
reasonably well, I saw the Notre Dame quarterback bless
himself. Sure enough, on this critical third down play, the
referee did the same thing. My fears really got out of hand
when there was a fumble near our bench and the referee
dived down into the middle of the pile and screamed, "I've
got it . . . it's our ball."

Bear Bryant is another coach with a dry wit, but he's all
business on the football field. He commands the respect of
his players and gets the very utmost out of his talent. When
the Bear was coaching at Texas A & M his Aggies went into
the last game of the season with the Southwest Conference
title practically wrapped up. His team was leading Baylor
20–14 with just fifty-five seconds to play, and A & M had the
ball at the Baylor 9. Bear was more interested in running
out the clock than in putting another score on the board,

so he sent word to his quarterback to merely fall on the ball, since the other team had used all its time outs.

The last remaining chance Baylor had for victory was to force a fumble and regain possession, so the Bears put all eleven men up on the line. When Bryant's quarterback saw the defensive setup he couldn't resist the chance to try to score. He figured a little swing pass to the outside would accomplish that, and doggoned if he didn't call it. He lofted the ball toward the sidelines and out of nowhere came a Baylor defensive back—one of the conference's top dash men—picked off the ball, and started flying down the field for the touchdown that would tie the game and set up the conversion that would knock Texas A & M out of the championship.

Like most quarterbacks, the young man from A & M was not the lightning-fast type. But somehow, he lit out after the man with the ball, made up some fifteen yards and tackled him from behind at the Aggies' 14-yard line as the gun sounded. It was at least a minor miracle.

After the game, newsmen asked the Aggie quarterback how it was humanly possible for him to catch up to the Baylor player who was a great deal faster and who already had such a big head start. The quarterback had a logical answer:

"You fellows don't know Coach Bryant like I do. This Baylor fellow was only running for a touchdown. I was running for my life."

I just don't know what my life would have been like had it not been for football. It's provided my family with a decent living, given us a chance to travel, to work with the best young men in America, and enabled us to laugh. I could laugh even in 1969 when we won only four games.

That was the year we tried the triple-option, but it really was a quadruple option the way we did it. We could hand the ball off, pitch it out, pass it, or just let it lie there on the ground where we dropped it. The object of the triple option was to by-pass the defensive tackle and end in the flow of the play without blocking them. That was easy for us. We never blocked them anyhow.

When I was working in the mines, I wanted a college education, but it just didn't seem possible at the time. I used to sit in the mine waiting for the motormen to bring in some empty cars. I was working with a fellow I had gone to high school with, even though he was a couple of years older and had more experience in the mines than I. Fred had a slight impediment of speech, and he was married, and he, too, had a dream. As I wanted a college education, all Fred ever wanted was enough money to buy the best tailor-made suit ever seen in Barnesboro, Pennsylvania. Well, I was lucky. I got out of the mines and went on to college, and you know the rest. Fred stayed there in the mines.

Years later, they had a "Duffy Daugherty Day" back in Barnesboro, and it was great seeing my old friends. I learned that after sixteen years in the mines, Fred also had realized his life's ambition. He finally had saved three hundred bucks that he thought he could spare from his family, and he went to the only tailor in Barnesboro, Adam Adamoski, and told Adam he wanted the finest suit ever made in Barnesboro.

So after several fittings, Adam pronounced the work completed and Fred walked proudly down 10th Street in his custom-made duds. There are just two main streets in Barnesboro, 10th and Philadelphia, and as Fred got to the corner he passed his friend Gus Bush. Fred was fairly bursting with pride as he asked his friend, "Well, Gus, how do you like my tailor-made suit?"

Gus examined the outfit, said it seemed like nice material but noted that the left sleeve seemed too short. Freddie raced back to Adam Adamoski's.

"Now, Fred," said Adam, "this is the finest piece of material ever to come into Cambria County. For the next week or ten days you're just gonna have to pull down on that sleeve and it'll work itself into shape."

Fred leaves the shop and starts back down the street and he's not gone five minutes when he passes another old friend, George Jividen, and right away Georgie wants to know, "Fred, what happened to you? Did you hurt your arm?"

"No," Fred replied. "You see, I just got this tailor-made suit. Paid three hundred bucks for it down at Adam Adamoski's. It's the finest material ever to come into Cambria County, but the sleeve is a little short but if I hold it down, in a week or so I'll have it just right."

"That's fine," said Georgie, "but what about that lapel? It shouldn't be sticking up like that."

Sure enough, the left lapel was sticking up like a sprouting lily, so Fred raced back to Adam's and demanded an explanation.

As usual, Adam had a ready explanation for that, too.

"Look, just hold your chin on the lapel and that'll straighten it out. In a week or ten days you'll have the best looking tailor-made suit ever seen in Western Pennsylvania."

Out Freddie goes again, and this time he runs into Chubby Mitchell who wanted to know if Freddie had been in some kind of accident. Once more Freddie explains the whole thing and Chubby nods in understanding. "Fine," he said, "but that crotch is way too long."

By this time Freddie is hotter than a two-dollar pistol, and he slams the door at Adam Adamoski's and rips into Adam, "By God, this is the last straw, Adam. You made the sleeve too long, the lapel sticks up, and now the crotch is too long!"

Adam gets a little belligerent himself and snorts back at Freddie, "This is the last time I want you in here bothering me. You know how to fix that crotch as well as I do. Just pull up on it, and remember to keep your chin on the lapel and pull down on that sleeve. After a week or so you're gonna have the dandiest suit this town has ever seen."

Poor old Freddie slams the door behind him, gets in gear once more and heads up 10th Street when he passes two strangers. Both stared long and hard at the awkward figure making his way toward Philadelphia Avenue, and one finally says to the other, "I wonder what's wrong with that poor devil?"

"I have no idea," said the other, "but I'll tell you one thing. That sure is a fine suit he's wearing."

The Changing Face of Football

The athlete of the '70s is more sophisticated, more aware, more sensitive, and a more complete human being than at any time in history.

As the game has changed, so have the people who play it and coach it. The people who watch it have changed, too. Today's athlete is far more gifted than those of yesteryear. He's bigger, faster, and stronger and can do more things, I don't care what the old-timers say. There are lots of reasons for that—better diet, better medication, fewer childhood ailments, better facilities, more opportunities. Perhaps in some ways he is less dedicated, and that compounds the already-staggering pressures of coaching.

In earlier times, the coach could operate much like an old-fashioned father. He simply told his children what to do, and they did it without questioning him. It was incomprehensible that they would ask "why?" It was none of their damned business why. He said it, and that was the law of the land. Coaches had pretty much that same kind of authority.

Attitudes toward athletes have changed greatly. A few years back a campus survey showed that students no longer hold athletes in awe. They no longer are the "big men on campus." That hero stuff is all but gone. The athlete sometimes is regarded with what you might call enthusiastic indifference. Sometimes he's even disdained. I think all this is natural and in keeping with our changing times across the land. The same problems that confront us as a nation, as a community, face us on the campus and, for that matter, on the football field.

Let's talk first about the so-called "black problem."

At Michigan State, it never was a problem. We had people who tried to make it a problem, but I can honestly say I never had a racial problem of any kind. I was the first coach who actively recruited blacks out of the South. And I didn't go after them because they were black but because they were good football players. I never thought of those players as being different, and they knew it.

That's why I was so dismayed when the story broke in the late 1960s that we were having trouble with our black athletes. There was some problem on campus as there was all across the country but it had nothing whatsoever to do with football.

There was a so-called Black Student Alliance on campus and there were some football players in that group. Their concern was that there was not enough black involvement within the framework of the university—secretaries, administrators, cheerleaders, you name it. We had already hired a black assistant coach, but the BSA had some grievances in other sports. The committee took the matter to our athletic director, Biggie Munn, and told him frankly that unless meaningful steps were taken—and right now—they would boycott all spring sports. That meant spring football, too.

The players came to me and asked for my reaction. I

guess it was predictable. My rules always were very simple. If a player had more than two unexcused absences, he was automatically off the team. The players were caught in the middle. They wanted to stand firm with their brothers yet they didn't want to lose out in football. So their spokesman asked if I could bend the rule this one time, but I refused. They knew, and I knew, that all this had nothing to do with football. But the press and the public wouldn't know that.

Our black athletes missed one day of practice. I made no announcement of any kind, but everyone knew if they missed one more, that was it. President Hannah saved the day, as he so frequently did. Spring practice rules permit four practice days per week. Dr. Hannah asked if I could excuse the blacks from the next practice. My answer to him was that I thought that would work to the detriment of the entire squad. He said he thought the issue could be resolved if the black athletes could meet with our faculty representative, Dr. John Fuzak. The compromise solution was to call off practice for one day for everyone while the summit meeting took place. The problems were aired and solved, and practice resumed. Everyone was back on the field, and that was the extent of our so-called "black problem."

There was a much-publicized incident involving Charles (Bubba) Smith, our great All-American, that led some people to believe there was a long-standing feud between the two of us. Bubba was a great, if difficult, star for us, and after he got out of school, his younger brother Tody came to Michigan State. Tody was never really happy at MSU, he was hurt, and finally wound up at Southern California where he did very well. Bubba was quoted as saying that

we treated his brother unfairly. But let's go back to the beginning because the story involves almost everyone in the
Smith family.

Bubba's father was a very successful high school football
coach in Beaumont, Texas. We had tried to recruit Bubba's
older brother, Willie Ray, but he wound up at Iowa. Willie
Ray wasn't happy there and eventually left school. So when
Bubba was a senior in high school, Mr. Smith called me and
asked if we'd "take a chance on my boy Bubba and try to
make a man out of him."

"You're his father and you've been his coach," I told Mr.
Smith. "If you can't make a man out of him, how do you
expect me to?"

We agreed to try because of Mr. Smith's pleadings, not
to mention Bubba's exceptional talents. When Bubba came
to college, he spent more time running laps than he did
doing anything else. The coaches couldn't get Bubba to
work like the rest of the team. Burt Smith, who's now
MSU's athletic director, had to stay on Bubba's back all the
time for loafing. In the spring of Bubba's freshman year,
he joined the varsity workouts, and all the coaches were
apprehensive because he had been so tough to handle. Hank
Bullough was a plenty tough guy and he was in charge of
our defensive line, so Bubba Smith became his responsibility.
But Hank couldn't seem to motivate the big guy either, and
one day he threw his hands up and tossed the problem
squarely into my lap.

"Put him on the scouting team and forget about him,"
was my solution.

That's just what we did, but in a few days Bubba came
into my office and wanted to know why he wasn't getting
"a chance." I told him, "Bubba, you're either going to be

a great All-American for Michigan State, or you're not going
to play a single minute of varsity football. It's as simple as
that. You refuse to go all out, and if you don't give a hundred per cent, you don't play for me."

Bubba was destroyed. "But you know I'm better than all
those guys out there."

"I know that, Bubba, and that's what makes all this such
a tragedy. Having ability is one thing. You have to use it,
all the time."

Then I told him that if he would rather leave school, I'd
try to get someone else to take a chance on him. Instead, he
asked for another chance. So we threw him into a scrimmage against our first team. Right off the bat, end Dick
Flynn and tackle Rahn Bentley got Bubba in a two-on-one
situation and drove the big fellow about five yards back into
the ground. Bubba was so riled up he kicked one of the
players in the head. And Bubba wore size 15½ shoes. The
blow could have broken a man's neck.

I swear to God this is the only time in all my years of
coaching that I ever put my hands on a player in anger. I
was so damned mad I jumped on Bubba's chest and started
pounding his head into the ground. Of course, I got on him
when he was down, proving I'm not totally stupid. I
grabbed him by the shoulder pads and kept bouncing him
up and down. He could have twisted me in two, but I
guess he was so stunned he just took it. Finally a couple of
coaches pulled me off him, and I was sputtering and raving
and I told Bubba to get off the field and off the squad.

"There's no place in football for someone like you," I
thundered.

Bubba sulked a while on the sidelines then wandered
into the locker room. He was waiting for me after practice.

"Coach, give me one more chance and that's all I'll ever ask of you."

I decided to try him one more time. Just a day or so later we were scrimmaging and one of the offensive linemen was doing a good job keeping Bubba out. Coach Bullough screamed at Bubba and asked him why he didn't rip through there. Bubba pointed to where I was standing. "The offensive man is holding me, but I'm afraid to belt him because of what the man over there might do."

Well, we got that mess straightened around in short order, and from then on Bubba went on to utilize all his skills. He made All-America in both his junior and senior years. Bubba was one of the most charming con men I've ever met. He always challenged me a little, though, even after that flareup. For example, we had a rule that players couldn't park their cars around the stadium. They lived in a dormitory and I figured an athlete could walk the two hundred yards to the stadium. When Bubba came back to school for his senior year he had a big new car with "Bubba" written on it. I suspected that one of the pro teams had given it to him, and I was determined to get to the bottom of it. A national sports magazine inferred that one of our alumni had given him the car. Bubba told me his father went to the bank down in Beaumont and took out a loan for him. I not only called Mr. Smith, but the bank. Sure enough, he was telling me the truth.

One day I was informed Bubba had driven that shiny new car to practice and parked it right outside the stadium. I walked into the locker room as the team was dressing after practice. I blew my whistle to get everyone's attention, then said,

"Charles Smith, you have precisely five minutes to get

that car out of there, or you can get in it and drive straight back to Beaumont."

He never said a word. He did move the car.

Ours was a strange relationship. At times he would be very sullen, at other times very personable. Ofttimes after games he'd rush up and hug and kiss me. After he went into the pros and Tody was having his difficulties at MSU, Bubba spouted off about Tody getting shabby treatment. Tody's case was unique. First, he had to play in the shadow of his older brother. He complained of his foot hurting, but our medical people couldn't find anything really wrong with him. Our coaches and some of the players always felt Tody was dogging it.

Tody was unhappy and contacted both Houston and Southern Cal, but was turned down at both places. He kept complaining about his foot, so we finally sent him to a specialist at Ann Arbor, Michigan, and he found that Tody really did have a problem with a tendon. He still wanted to leave Michigan State, so I called John McKay and he agreed to accept Tody at Southern Cal. Tody still had two years of eligibility remaining, and he had a great career with the Trojans.

I had no idea what the feeling would be when Bubba and I met face to face. But everything was fine. Just before the 1973 season I was in California doing a film for ABC Sports and all of a sudden two big hands were wrapped around me. In one of the hands was a lighted cigarette. I said, "This can't be Bubba Smith, because the Bubba I know doesn't smoke."

We had a good long chat and Bubba said, "Coach, I don't know how you ever put up with me."

I don't know either, but I'm glad I did.

It's difficult to keep an entire squad happy. Winning helps, but you can only play so many people. A baseball manager can play only nine, so he has sixteen sitting on the bench and some of them are gonna be grumbling. Anyone who's really content sitting on a bench is either a fool or downright lazy. In football, you have sixty or more players, and only twenty-two can play regularly. That's one of the hardest jobs in coaching, seeing to it that an entire squad is as much of a unit as possible.

Like I said, football and the players have changed. Part of the change in football is the by-product of the tremendous pressures from recruiting, because of the necessity to win, in order to fill every seat in the stadium. With twenty and thirty or more schools going after an exceptional athlete, and having to worry about grades and a summer job and a thousand other things, little wonder the young men changed, and little wonder that coaches everywhere violated the spirit of the rules.

The distractions for our students are much greater than ever. Young people are much more involved in every facet of campus life. They're more interested in the world about them and that's good. Some of our finest citizens on campus are members of the athletic teams. The leadership and discipline they need for excellence in athletic competition are the same things that produce good human beings. Generally, today's athlete isn't content to be just a jock. He thinks highly of himself as a total human being, as an involved and interested person.

This may sound incongruous, but while today's athlete is more willing to lift weights to improve his strength, he is a more diversified individual and thus he lacks that single-mindedness that athletes used to have. He simply has less intensity about football, and he strongly resents the strong-back-weak-mind concept that people in the past have had about football players. The game of football simply isn't an all-consuming thing to most players of today.

Take this business of long hair. I think this illustrates what today's athlete is all about. When long hair became fashionable for men, the athlete wanted to have long hair, too, because it was very important to him to be identified with the masses. Athletes no longer want to be singled out. They want to do their thing in sports, but they want to look like everyone else and to be treated like everyone else. Personally, I never saw any correlation between short hair and victory. The only rule I ever had was that the players had to be clean and well-groomed.

Ordering players to cut their hair doesn't mean a coach has discipline. The only kind of discipline worth a dime is the self-imposed discipline that a team puts upon itself because it is imbued with a desire to excel and a readiness to accept a few simple rules for the good of the team. Discipline, to me, was convincing a team that it had to be in superior physical condition, willing to push itself almost beyond the limits of physical endurance. Discipline means getting players not only willing but anxious to punish themselves. The truly great player will push himself when he's dog tired because he understands that only through that kind of effort do you attain physical and mental toughness.

Anyone can accomplish something when he's fresh. But the person who can press on even when he arrives at the absolute limit of his endurance is the one who wins for you when times are most trying. This is where the emotional takes over from the physical, and it's a keenly pitched emotional team that attains physical toughness that enables it to extract critical victories.

Someone wrote a long time ago that adversity introduces a man to himself. It's easy to be nice when times are good, but the true test of a person is how he reacts under stress. I've always felt that a well-balanced person is one who strives for and prepares for success and achievement, but at the same time doesn't become unglued when he faces failure instead.

Maybe we could compare it to the story of the man and wife who went to a Halloween masquerade party disguised as a cow—he was the front end, she the rear. They had quite a bit to drink and decided it'd be better to walk home rather than risk driving. They took a short cut across a field and suddenly in the moonlight they spotted a big bull. As they stood there in their cow's costume, the bull began to charge.

"What are we gonna do?" pleaded the wife, and the husband retorted,

"Well, dear, I'm gonna munch on some grass. I'd recommend that you brace yourself."

If I Had My Way

As long as we have scoreboards, we will have controversy.

But some of the controversy in college football today could be eliminated. All it takes is a little common sense, but someone said long ago that common sense is very uncommon. There are ways to eliminate a lot of the petty bickering, ways to improve the game of football, and ways to make it more interesting for fans, players, and coaches.

Last season, the bickering centered around two issues: Which team should go to the Rose Bowl, and which team should be ranked number one. The arguments rage on even today. But there is a way to settle one and completely avoid the other.

This business of debating which team from the Big Ten should have gone to the Rose Bowl should never have come up. All the back-biting and sniping was stupid. The confrontation involving athletic directors was unnecessary and avoidable. Had the Big Ten acted with any degree of common sense and objectivity, the conference would have had the team picked from the game between Ohio State and Michigan, just in case the game ended in a tie.

Ohio and Michigan entered the final game of the regular

season unbeaten and untied. Ohio State was ranked No. 1 in the nation. The Buckeyes had been No. 1 most of the season. Five times in six years these two teams had met for the same stakes—the championship of the Big Ten and a trip to Pasadena. Theirs is a classic series, a game almost annually featured on national television, a game with every single ingredient for greatness, and a game in which legends are born.

When they tied 10–10, most everyone assumed Michigan would be selected for the Rose Bowl, since Ohio State had gone to Pasadena the year before (and up until last year, the Big Ten exercised the no-repeat rule that precluded a team making two straight trips to the Rose Bowl). Matter of fact, I was part of the ABC Sports television broadcast crew doing the game, and I speculated on national television that Michigan would get the nod, on the basis of the Wolverines' stirring comeback from a 10–0 deficit and their domination of play in the second half. Michigan just had to be the sentimental favorite because even though the game ended in a deadlock, the Wolverines had the upper hand after the early going.

Now, before the kickoff I would have voted for Ohio State because the Buckeyes had been No. 1, they had a more impressive record, and they had fared better against common opponents. After the game, even Ohio State coach Woody Hayes figured Michigan would get the vote of the conference athletic directors.

The Pacific-8 Conference has a sensible system, and the Pac-8 had predetermined that should the UCLA-Southern California game end in a tie, UCLA would get the Rose Bowl bid. I'm not advocating using statistics to determine such a thing because you just can't go on the basis of yards

gained or first downs. It's been proven that the team with
the upper hand in statistics wins only 53 per cent of the
time, but the team with the fewest turnovers wins 95 per
cent of the time.

In the Big Ten, the faculty representatives put in the rules
that the athletic directors had to follow. I know for certain
that the directors and coaches NEVER were in sympathy
with the no-repeat rule. The faculty people argued constantly that it was academically unsound for a team to go to
the Rose Bowl two years running, but they could never come
up with a sensible answer when you confronted them with
the fact that West Coast teams like Stanford and Southern
California and UCLA do it—and what's wrong with their
classroom records? So the Big Ten athletic directors voted
for Ohio State and the powder keg was ignited. Their vote
proved that the athletic directors never liked the no-repeat
rule. It proved, too, that most of the people in the conference felt that over the long haul, Ohio State was a "more
representative" team than Michigan.

Michigan folks yelped "foul." Coach Bo Schembechler
had strong criticism for Big Ten commissioner Wayne
Duke, implying that Duke influenced some votes for Ohio
State. I can understand Bo's disappointment. He's an in-
tense and volatile man and a hugely successful coach. He
knows how to motivate his players, and his teams are always well-prepared and technically sound. It was an awful
letdown for Bo, his players, and the Michigan fans. I can
even understand Bo's outburst at the commissioner, even
though it never is wise even to hint that the commissioner
might not be totally impartial.

Knowing Woody Hayes as I do, had the situation been
totally reversed I think garrulous old Woody would have

kicked up just as big a storm. I don't know what Michigan
would have done against Southern California had the
Wolverines made the trip West, but Ohio State's convincing
triumph made them jump for joy in Ohio, lopped a few
beads of sweat off the brows of some athletic directors, and
restored a tiny bit of pride to the Big Ten.

But why did Michigan's Wolverines have to sit home on
New Year's Day? Why should the Big Ten be restricted
to one bowl game, and be married to the Pac-8? Not infre-
quently in recent years the Big Eight and the Southeastern
conferences have had four and five teams in post-season
bowl games. But the Big Ten has an ancient, asinine pact
with the Pacific-8 Conference that ties both leagues to the
granddaddy of the bowl games. The Rose Bowl is great.
I've been there and it's everything they say it is, and a whole
lot more. But it's not the end of the world, and there's no
reason on God's green earth why the Big Ten runner-up, or
another worthy team for that matter, should be prevented
from taking part in another bowl game.

The Big Ten has made some long-overdue progress in
the last couple of years in tossing out the no-repeat rule and
getting in stride on red shirting. But the faculty representatives are still living in the Stone Age when it comes to their
bowl policy. At a time when there's a great need for more
money in the colleges, additional bowl games would provide
more revenue for the schools, more incentive for the players,
and more interest for the fans.

More than ten years ago I first advocated a play-off series
to determine a true national champion. I still believe in my
basic plan, although I have modified it of late. Having a
national play-off is even more sensible and practical than it
was when I first proposed it. Just look back as far as the 1973

season. AP selected Notre Dame the No. 1 team in the nation, and conducted its final balloting among writers and sports broadcasters AFTER the bowl games had been decided. UPI picked Alabama, but the UPI board of coaches voted BEFORE the bowl games. So what happened? Notre Dame knocked off Alabama 24 to 23 in the Sugar Bowl and we wound up with two champions. Meanwhile, Penn State and Miami of Ohio wound up unbeaten and untied with practically nothing to show for it.

College football is the greatest game ever from the standpoint of spectator appeal—but only because of the skills of the players and the ingenuity of the coaches. If we could just get the governing bodies of sports to leap headlong into the twentieth century, there's a better-than-even chance we could make the game more interesting.

A national play-off would stir tremendous new interest in the college game. Under my plan, the season would be extended for only four teams—and we could increase fan interest 25 per cent and be able to crown, every year, a legitimate champion and thus rid ourselves of all that "mythical" junk.

The idea first popped into my head when I was asked in a survey if I felt the national polls were accurate and good for football. My answer was no and yes. They're not at all accurate, but they are good for the game.

I'm convinced that a national play-off would be tremendously stimulating for the game, the people in it, and the people watching it. After all, why should our colleges have national play-offs in hockey and basketball and baseball and track and field, but not in football? It makes no sense at all.

Here's my plan: I'm for selecting four teams from around the country to take part in a post-season series. Now, I'm not for disturbing the present bowl game set-up—not in the least. Matter of fact, my plan would enhance the attractiveness of those established classics. After all the bowl games are played, a blue-ribbon committee appointed by the National Collegiate Athletic Association would then select the four best teams in the land to take part in the play-offs.

There would be just three games—two semi-final contests and then the Super Bowl of college football. You could use the sites of the four major bowl games—in Pasadena, Dallas, New Orleans, and Miami—as alternating sites for the play-offs. The first two games would be played the first weekend after the concluding bowl games—probably around January 8, or the Saturday following New Year's Day. You know, you wouldn't really need a week for preparation, because the participating teams already would be taking part in bowl games and would be in excellent condition.

Following the two semi-final games, the players then could go back to their campuses—since most schools have indoor facilities for working out if the weather is foul—then return for the showdown game. The academicians are concerned, I know, about the student-athletes spending too much time away from campus, so under this plan they could return to class, then fly out to the finals the Friday before the last game. The finals would be played on the Saturday before the Super Bowl.

Many colleges are in the middle of holiday vacations at that time, anyway, so any classroom disruption would be a tiny one.

Can you imagine what an attractive television package these three games would make? I'm no expert on high finance in television, but it's my guess the three-game deal would go for at least five million dollars. You could take that money and divide it equally among the 120-odd major colleges and universities playing top-grade football. That would mean $40,000 for the badly depleted athletic budget of each school. The participating teams, of course, would get a great deal more money out of their shares of the box office receipts.

There's just no way it could miss. I don't see a possible weakness in it. In fact, I'm so certain of its success—financially and artistically—that I'd like to be the promoter of the whole thing.

As for the committee, I'd select a combination of coaches and athletic directors with the wisdom and integrity to select the finest teams in the country. You'd have certain guidelines, to be sure. Maybe you'd have to eliminate a team with a defeat, but there are ways to do it.

If I were asked to appoint the committee right this minute, I'd probably select either a coach or athletic director from each of the major conferences and add some representatives from the major independents. These are men of integrity who could objectively analyze the top teams and do the job properly, because their only interest would be in selecting the very finest teams for this classic event.

For example, I'd pick Moose Krause of Notre Dame, Don Canham of Michigan, Bear Bryant of Alabama, either Darrell Royal of Texas or Frank Broyles of Arkansas, Joe Paterno of Penn State, Fred Miller of Arizona State, Dick Shrider of Miami of Ohio, John McKay of Southern California, Earle Edwards of North Carolina State, Bob Devaney of Nebraska. I'm just pulling these names off the top of my head, but they'd be good ones, and there are others who would be just as effective and every bit as conscientious.

This whole concept would mean better merchandising of an already-great game, it would determine a true champion, it would produce needed revenue, and it would not be disruptive academically. Let's face it, college football is right in the thick of the battle for the entertainment dollar, and we must realize that we are competitors with professional football even though we have to live with the pro game. We must do the best possible job of projecting the image of college football—and right now we're not doing that job properly. Centuries ago there was a famous line about not hiding our light under a bushel. Having a national collegiate football play-off would bring our thing right out into the open for all to see.

You know, the minute you announced the site of the play-off games, the tickets would be sold out a year in advance—just as they do now in college basketball.

You wouldn't get any argument about this plan from the bowl games, because it does not infringe on them. They'd go about their business in the same way with the same method of selecting their teams. The educators can't complain now because you'd still retain the campus atmosphere and return the players to their home schools between games.

I had thought previously about other plans—one of them involving the four major bowl games as play-off sites, with eight teams taking part in the championship runoff. But the proposal to have four teams competing in three games AFTER all the bowl games have been played is without a weakness. I think Walter Byers, the erudite executive director of the NCAA, would endorse this one. His is an important but a thankless job—trying to keep all the colleges and universities happy—but I know he'd be in favor of

anything that helps the game and the people who participate in it and does not disrupt the academic processes.

You know, back in the mid-sixties, Michigan State was
not permitted to go to the Rose Bowl game twice in a row,
even though our Spartans won the Big Ten championship
in 1966. One of our victims that year was Purdue. We beat
the Boilermakers 41–20 after leading 35–7, but Purdue was
selected to go to the Rose Bowl. Purdue played a Southern
California team that had been walloped 51–0 by Notre
Dame. Purdue won the Rose Bowl game 14–13, and if you
think it was a weak attraction, consider that the crowd for
that contest was the largest in the history of the Rose Bowl
up to that time.

We also could have a better, and more believable rating
system. I'm sure neither wire service will agree, but it just
makes good sense to abandon both polls and come up with
a single rating system with a fairer method of voting. Let's
face it, whether it's writers and broadcasters or coaches
doing the voting, no one can possibly see all the top teams
in the country.

My proposal is to put an equal number of coaches and
writers-broadcasters on one panel, with equal representation
for every sector of the country. I think a power rating would
help, too. You surely should get more points for beating Alabama than you'd get for beating a lesser foe. I'm not down-
grading any school, but we all know some teams historically
are a lot tougher than others. If one Big Ten team plays
Nebraska, Southern Cal, and Notre Dame in non-conference
activity, that team should be given more consideration in
the ratings than the Big Ten team that has Navy, Duke, and
Virginia on its schedule. I like the way they judge diving,

on the degree of difficulty. A man should get more points for doing a two-and-one-half gainer than for a simple half-twist. Nebraska and Oklahoma have been extremely powerful in the Big Eight for the last several years. Why should one of them be severely penalized for losing to the other, when a lesser team gets a lot of credit for going unscathed through a much more modest schedule? We might even get computers to help establish some rating system. If we can use them to help us put folks on the moon and get 'em back again, we surely could find a way to have computers help us rate football teams.

Some of my colleagues have urged formation of a so-called super conference. I'm totally against that. Just look at the Big Ten, for example. Right now you'd put Ohio State and Michigan into a super conference. But what about the others? In recent seasons, Michigan State was the dominant force in the league. Before that, Iowa was a prime contender for national championship honors. Purdue, Illinois, and Wisconsin all have had superior teams in the not-too-distant past. In the Southeastern Conference, you'd have to consider not only Alabama, but LSU, Tennessee, Georgia, and Mississippi, because in recent years each of these schools has produced what you'd call super teams. A super conference just isn't feasible.

There is an alternative, though. The NCAA could create more competitive games, more thought-provoking confrontations between powerful teams. Schedules now are drawn up some ten years ahead of time. That's ridiculous, because no one can foresee the quality of the teams nor the rules under which all of us will be operating. I think the National Collegiate Athletic Association should tear up all schedules made for more than three years ahead of time.

If you imposed a three-year scheduling limit, you could
create more classics like Alabama vs Oklahoma, Ohio
State vs Notre Dame, Tennessee vs Texas, and so on. An
important by-product would be the provincialism that
affects the game and its fans. The schedules being drawn
up today will be played by little boys who right now are in
the second grade, dipping little girls' braids into inkwells.

Now, another proposal, if you will. Let's use tie breakers
in college football. Not in every game, mind you, but when
a conference title is at stake, or when you're in a play-off or
a bowl game, why settle for a tie? Someone once said that a
tie is like kissing your sister. It surely is no more exciting
than that. Here's my proposal: When a significant game
ends in a deadlock, give the players a double time out (even
a 10-minute rest is too much because of the danger of the
players cooling off) and then let 'em go at it again, starting
with a regulation coin flip. The team winning the coin toss
would have the option of receiving or defending a particular
goal. Some commentators remark about a team electing to
kick-off, but I've never known a team that elected to kickoff. What they do is select a goal because of a decided wind
advantage. When we had our great defensive teams in the
mid-sixties, we'd always opt for the wind advantage if it
was a good one. We had enough confidence that our defense
could stop the other team and take the ball away from them.
Besides, we had a good kickoff man, and we generally
wound up with good field position. It also gives you a
tremendous psychological advantage if you give a team the
ball, then take it away from them.

But back to the tie breaker—the first team to score either
a field goal or a touchdown would be the winner. It's a
simple formula and wouldn't take that much more out of

the players. Besides, they don't like ties, either. The name of the game, remember, is win.

Another thing that would help the college game is putting the goal post back on the goal line. Why in the devil should we play every facet of the game except the kicking game on a field 100 yards long—then use 120 yards for the kicking part of it? It makes no sense at all. We've already incorporated the 2-point conversion into college ball and putting the goal post on the goal line would give added incentive to going for it.

In the professional ranks, the goal post is on the goal line, and so the extra point is almost automatic. In college, every extra point actually amounts to a twenty-yard field goal— and some of the pros miss that kind.

Some other suggestions: If a ball is kicked into the end zone, let's give it to the receiving team at the 35-yard line instead of at the 20. The deadest play in football without a doubt is a kick that isn't returned.

Let's put the foot back into football. Years ago, kicking instructors used to tour the colleges. Today, kicking the ball out of bounds is a lost art. Why not penalize a team for kicking a ball into the end zone? You'd force teams to train their kickers and ere long you'd have a whole new dimension to the game.

I'm in favor of a change in scoring as well. Why should a team get 3 points for a nineteen-yard field goal and the same number of points for a fifty-yard field goal? Let's award 3 points for anything up to thirty-five yards and 4 points for anything beyond that. And when a team misses a field goal, return the ball to the line of scrimmage, instead of placing it on the 20. That would discourage teams from trying unrealistic field-goal attempts—but then, realism hasn't always been part of the makeup of the gentlemen who write the rules. An alternative is to bring the ball out to the 35 after unsuccessful field goals. That might simplify it for fans, officials, and particularly the coaches.

I've heard some sentiment for utilizing television's instant replay technique as an aid to officials. The officials very likely would scorn the idea, but they don't make the rules either. No question about it, sometimes officials do need a little help, and I'm one coach who has volunteered his services from time to time. I have learned, though, through my brief telecasting experience that instant replays prove the officials are right more frequently than the fans, and coaches for that matter, generally think.

There is an economic factor to consider. It'd be tremendously expensive, and you surely couldn't have it for every game. But most significant games are televised, so the equipment is readily available. On top of that, consider the fact that many, many major universities have their own television facility. I would not be opposed to using instant replay to assist officials in key games. It could be of vital importance on the sideline pass (did the man have his feet in bounds or out?) and on pass receptions (did he catch it or trap it?).

The colleges today have a more exciting game than the pros. The pros argue that if they seem to be stereotyped, it's because their players are so proficient as to be robotlike. That's a bunch of garbage. The pros have a great game. Don't make any mistakes about that, and don't number Duffy Daugherty among the critics who say the Miami Dolphins' victory over the Minnesota Vikings in the Super Bowl last January was dull and routine. But the college game is a better, more wide-open game with greater spectator appeal than ever before.

The willingness of college coaches to develop running quarterbacks gives their game a dimension that the pros simply do not have. The college teams have double and triple options and put far more burden on the defense. It's a much more diversified game. Whether the pros will change gradually to more of a running quarterback system is debatable. Hank Stram of the Kansas City Chiefs speculated a couple of years ago that it would have to happen, but so far I haven't seen it.

You see, when a pro quarterback drops back into the pocket, or rolls out, or elects to scramble (or is forced to) he has to gain six or seven or eight yards before he's even back to the line of scrimmage. In college ball, the quarterback is but a whisper behind the line of scrimmage. Thus, he's more of an offensive threat. Because he's right on the line, he can cut off the pursuit and force the defensive end to tackle him—or he can pitch back to another runner. Or he can pass (unless he plays for Woody). If only because of the dimensions of the game involving the quarterback, the colleges play a better game for the folks who watch it.

Now—everyone's been griping about the increasingly heavy economic burdens in college athletics. Steps have been taken to resolve some of the problem, with all schools now restricted to thirty grants-in-aid each year for football. The Big Ten has been operating on this theory for years, but the new rule brings the rest of the country in line. That, plus adoption of the red-shirt rule, will put the Big Ten back where it rightfully belongs in big time football. But it won't happen until 1976 or 1977. It'll take the Big Ten that long to catch up, but the conference will be back, because of the geographical location of the schools, their proximity to the great high school talent in the large population centers.

Money will continue to be a problem, simply because football is charged with the responsibility of supporting almost every other athletic endeavor in the colleges and universities. At Michigan State, for example, we have thirteen varsity sports. Hockey might make a tiny bit of money and perhaps basketball breaks even, but king football has to support all the others. That's why even some of our thick-headed faculty representatives cannot kill football, because football is the sugar daddy and there are too many mouths to feed.

It Was Worth It

Today, the title is "assistant to the vice-president in charge of development."

What it means is that after all these years, I'm still out recruiting. But instead of recruiting an eighteen-year-old high school senior to come to Michigan State and get an education and play football, I'm trying to convince his father or his uncle to donate at least $10,000 to the university.

My job is to influence alumni and friends to join the President's Club, to recognize and to be receptive to the total needs of a great university. It has nothing to do with sports, really, except that a donor can earmark a gift for the athletic department if he wants, just as he can specify that the gift goes to the music or biology department.

Two things about my new assignment. First, I wouldn't have taken it if I felt the school simply created a cubbyhole for me to crawl into, if I felt MSU was just being nice to a gray-haired old football coach. Too, I wouldn't have taken the job if that's all I had to do. I know that job alone isn't enough to keep me busy or happy.

I walked away from coaching in the fall of 1972. I never had any intention of walking away from football. I didn't

miss the game so much the spring after I quit, because I
was busy on some golf tours, some speeches and clinics,
and in preparing myself for the first season of doing television football for ABC Sports. Also, I hadn't been away
from football all that long. But when autumn came, my guts
began to grind. Athletes get a great deal out of football, but
so do coaches.

It's a great thrill to watch young people develop and,
hopefully, to help them mature physically and emotionally.
Just to watch kids grow into men, to get better technically,
to improve their skills, and display the values that are necessary to a full and rich life—this is the real meaning of
coaching at its finest. By the very nature of my job, I was
asked thousands of times each year by anxious parents
whether I thought football was really good for their sons.

Football is human nature at its best, and sometimes at its
worst. Football is a game of emotion, laughter and tears,
heartbreak and exultation, frustration and comedy. You can
get things from competition that simply aren't available
anywhere else. I know what these values are because I've
seen them in thousands of young people.

It's been often said that football is a contact sport. Not
so. Football is a COLLISION sport; dancing is a contact
sport. On second thought, the way young people dance
today there's not a whole lot of contact. But the great contact in football is the personal, human contact you make
between human beings, contact not of the physical kind.
Edison said the formula for success was 1 per cent inspi-
ration and 99 per cent perspiration. I think that's true in
any profession, but it's a whole lot easier to demonstrate in
football.

I always told our young athletes that a willingness to work

hard was the key to our success. Athletes learn that they
must sacrifice things that are bigger than they as individuals.
We'd frequently recruit all-state halfbacks or all-state quarterbacks and fullbacks, and for the good of the team ask
them to play guard or tackle or defensive back or line-
backer. Personally, I've always considered it a great honor
to play in the line, since I played there myself, and let's face
it—anyone can carry a football. The darned thing weighs
only thirteen ounces.

A willingness to make a sacrifice for something bigger
than the individual is the most unselfish trait a man can
have. I've never known a truly happy person who hasn't
learned this lesson and made it a part of his life. I think if a
man learns that his church, his family, his community, and
his nation are more important than his own personal whims
and wishes, he's on the right road to contentment in life.
Football competition teaches a person to accept discipline,
to be willing to adhere to a few simple rules laid down for
the good of the team. It makes for good citizenship later in
life. We learn the value of giving the utmost of our God-
given talents. I told every squad I ever coached at Michigan
State all these things. Too, I told them that not everyone had
been blessed with equal ability. Some men are made bigger,
faster, stronger, and smarter than others—but not a single
one ever has a corner on dreams or desire or ambition.

I wrote each player several letters each year throughout
the summer. I'd send out the first letter in June and outline
some kind of conditioning program. In the second letter, in
July, I'd outline our goals, and our goals never varied an
ounce. We wanted to be champions of the Big Ten, go to
the Rose Bowl, and be the best college football team in the
country. I'd tell the squad something about our schedule

and our opponents and what we'd have to do to beat these teams. The third letter went out in August, and it was the invitation back to practice. In my final letter, I almost begged these fine young men to come back to campus imbued with the willingness to work hard, to accept discipline, to place the welfare of the team ahead of their individual aspirations, and, above all, to return with an overwhelming desire to excel and a willingness to give every ounce of ability at every practice and in each game. For the last fifteen years or so, I always enclosed the last four lines of an old poem that long has been a favorite of mine:

> If you can't be a highway, then be just a trail,
> If you can't be the sun, be a star;
> It isn't by size that you win or you fail;
> Be the best of whatever you are.

I had lots of chances to leave Michigan State. It's no secret that I was offered the Texas job before Darrell Royal took it. In fact, I recommended Darrell for that job. I was offered a lifetime contract as head coach and athletic director. I could have had the Southern California job before John McKay got it. There were lots of offers through the years, and as I look back, I probably carried my loyalty to Michigan State to extremes.

As for the pros—Don Kellett came to see me when I was coaching in the North-South Shrine Game and asked if I'd be interested in coaching the Baltimore Colts. Weeb Ewbank was coaching there then, and when a deal is presented like that, I always have the same answer. It's No. I said the same thing when I was asked about the Los Angeles Rams' job. Sid Gillman had the job then and I was watching the ponies at Santa Anita when I told the Rams' directors I wouldn't even discuss an offer with them. I was approached about the Green Bay job before Vince Lombardi took over.

The one pro deal I likely would have taken never got off the ground. A friend of mine inquired about buying the San Francisco 49ers from the Morabito family, but got turned down. I think I would have liked that deal.

The other job I was most linked with was the Notre Dame coaching job. It kept cropping up practically throughout my career at Michigan State. Here's the whole truth about the only time I was ever officially approached. It was in 1963, and we had won our opening game and were out West playing Southern Cal in the second game. It was a night game and we lost 13–10 after leading the thing 10–0. We should have won it, but Southern Cal scored in the final moments and it was a most disheartening trip back to the hotel. Soon after we returned to the Huntington Hotel, Dr. Hannah invited me to come up to his room.

"Put your feet up on the table and be comfortable, Duff," he instructed, and he had ordered a couple of beers. We talked about nothing important for a few minutes and then he said the nicest thing anyone ever uttered about me.

"Duffy," he began, "I like to think that the two men sitting in this room right now have done more for the history of Michigan State University than any two men in the history of the school. And I'm not talking about your football coaching, either. You know, there's never been a person who has made more friends for Michigan State than you."

Well, I don't have to tell you that when a man you respect that much comes out with something that nice, it just gives you the shakes all over. I didn't know what to say in response to him. It turned out I didn't have to say anything, and he went on to tell me that the president of Notre Dame had talked with him.

"The folks at South Bend want you to coach there next year even if you should lose every game this season. Now, I'm going to speak bluntly. I do not want you to leave Michigan State under any circumstances. I don't want you to go anywhere else. So you tell me, just what will it take to keep you at Michigan State?"

I told Dr. Hannah it wasn't a matter of money and never had been and never would be, because I've never used another offer as a wedge to get anything else. I told him that all I ever wanted to do was coach. So that's when he came up with the idea of giving me the title "Director of Football." All it meant was that I was to run the football department, and that included the hiring and firing of the coach. From that time, I had the authority to hire and fire myself. Now, I've always had considerable respect for my own coaching ability and I can say in all candor that Duffy the director of football never once contemplated firing Duffy the coach.

Ara Parseghian told me later that when the news came out that I had been given this new title, he then called Notre Dame and applied for the coaching job. Like lots of other people, he assumed the Notre Dame job was all locked up for me. Notre Dame had just fired Joe Kuharich and was using Huge Devore as an interim coach.

There were other times when influential alumni of Notre Dame came to see me about some possibilities, but it was strictly on an unofficial basis. Notre Dame is too classy and too ethical to do it any other way.

My relationship with John Hannah is the most treasured of all those I have formed in nineteen years as a head coach.

He has been a man of total integrity with the ability to objectively analyze every situation. If something made good sense, and if it was good for the university, he'd fight your battles right alongside you. He was such a great leader and good example that no one could ever doubt his motives. His word was all anyone ever needed.

He saw to it that his people had the tools to compete on equal footing, so while he was running the show we had an ample budget for recruiting, and enough money to hire talented assistants. But when he left, the leadership was gone, internal bickering and unhappiness surfaced because we no longer had those tools or the backing and encouragement of the administration. All of us could feel it slipping. We realized that our chances of keeping pace with the teams we had to beat were being minimized by restrictive rules and by people who didn't come close to sharing Dr. Hannah's enthusiasm, or close to having his drive for excellence and his awareness of the total situation. From the time he left, the way thus was established for me to go. Sometimes I think I should have gone out a year or two earlier, but with my eternal optimism I kept thinking I could pull off a miracle one more time. But it never happened. And waiting for miracles grinds the nerves.

When the administration asked me to stay on with the university after my decision to quit, I was asked what I wanted to do. My answer was that it would have to be meaningful to me and to the school. I never wanted a token job. I've seen some tragic things happen to coaches who have been put on a shelf created for them. They quickly lose their spirit and their zest for living. There's enough ego and ham in every coach to make it difficult to totally withdraw from the limelight and the things that have been fun for us. Sure, there are times when a fellow would like not to be noticed, but I'm sure the attention and recognition get to be important when you've enjoyed some success in the major leagues.

Being asked to be a part of the ABC Television Network college football telecasts helped solve a major dilemma for me—I didn't have to divorce myself from the game and the fine young men who play it and the nice people who coach it.

My first year in the broadcast booth was a little scary. In all the years I coached there was precious little time for watching football on television. We played on Saturdays and usually watched our own game films on Sunday. I think the main difficulty I had was in not being able to say all the things that came into my mind. The time restrictions simply made it impossible. As you're gathering your thoughts for a statement you believe is relevant, it's time to throw the microphone back to the play-by-play announcer. You see, in professional football, the players generally utilize about all the thirty seconds allotted between plays. But I've done research on the college game, and those kids put the ball into play on the average of once every sixteen seconds. So the play-by-play man has to set the formation and give any change in players. It doesn't leave time for as much chatter back and forth as I had thought it would. Dozens of times I found myself wanting to make a comment, but knowing there wasn't time to do it.

I do think, though, that I had one advantage over the game announcer. Having watched thousands of hours of football movies over the years, I found it was simpler for me to watch the monitor in the television booth, rather than concentrating on the action on the field all the time. I made it a practice to check the field as the teams came out of the huddle, so I could see the overall offensive formation and the defensive set. Then I immediately changed my view over to the monitor. The whole season was a ton of fun and it kept me associated with the greatest game in the world.

In my first year out of coaching, there were just two things I missed—mainly, the association with fine young men, and then the conducting of the games. A football game just doesn't happen, and victory isn't automatic. It doesn't matter how well prepared your team is, there are still decisions that have to be made every minute of the game. You have to properly utilize your personnel and plan ahead, much like in a chess match. You have to be constantly thinking about the down, the yardage, position on the field, the clock, your personnel, and the condition of your men. You also have to consider the score, the weather conditions, and the wind in planning ahead.

To be a successful coach, you have to be a successful recruiter. If you don't get the quality players, you can forget the rest. But even if you get your share of the blue-chippers, it's a lot more involved than just turning them loose on the field after one of those "win one for the Gipper" orations in the locker room.

I always got nervous before a game when I was coaching. The nervousness stayed with me in the broadcast booth. I've always been able to get keyed up at pep rallies, or when I hear a band playing a familiar march. I felt the same thing before each kickoff—even though I was high above the field in the television booth. The only difference was that I didn't care which team won. The viewers like to see points put on the board, so I always rooted for a well-played and a high-scoring game. But I hope I never lose sight of the fact that the folks are tuned in to watch a football game, not to hear Chris Schenkel, Bud Wilkinson, and Duffy Daugherty.

As I look back on the coaching, I realize it's possible for a man to stay in one place too long. I was at Michigan State a long time, seven years as an assistant and nineteen years as head coach. Conditions change, and so do people. We had great teams under Biggie Munn and some great teams when I was coaching. These teams were recruited with the help and encouragement of a friendly administration, a beautiful campus, outstanding facilities, and a strong conference. These became great selling points. For a long time, our facilities were comparable to any in the Big Ten. Our staff was happy, aggressive, and hard working, and recruiting rules were structured so we could accomplish something. We could bring prospects in frequently even though we could arrange to have just one paid visit. The prospects could spend weekends in the dormitories and get a taste of college life with other students. The most beautiful part of it all was that Dr. Hannah's office was always open, and prospects were always welcome. He was never too busy to talk with these young men, and I'm sure his attitude helped sway hundreds of young men to spend four years with us. We could play host to the young man's parents, the faculty was helpful, and we were successful. In recent years, recruiting rules were drastically altered so that it became necessary to have a well-organized alumni group, or individuals at the local level, to help out. It was essential for interested folks in the prospect's home town to take a special interest in the young man, in helping him make the decision to come to Michigan State.

Our alumni simply hadn't been accustomed to that. They had never had to do a lot of working and scraping that alumni from other schools were used to doing. They never had to help out much with the recruiting—and when we needed them, there was no way they could come through. I'm not saying they were unwilling—they simply were uneducated. They didn't know how to involve themselves.

As the rules became more strict, our alumni became more frustrated, the quality of our teams diminished, and our coaches became more harried. The Michigan State people were accustomed to letting Biggie and Duffy do it all. Now, if Michigan State is once again to excel as a national football power—and this is something I have spelled out to everyone concerned—the alumni and friends of the school are going to have to get their feet wet and their hands dirty. Ohio State and Michigan have been tremendously successful in recent seasons because both schools have strong, industrious, and well-organized alumni groups that help sell the Buckeyes and the Wolverines to the top prospects.

I should have left Michigan State five or six years before I finally walked out. Look around at the very successful coaches and you'll find that most of them have made a couple of moves. Bear Bryant was successful at Kentucky and Texas A & M before going to Alabama. Ara Parseghian moved from Miami to Northwestern to Notre Dame, Fritz Crisler from Princeton to Michigan, Dan Devine from Arizona State to Missouri to the NFL Green Bay Packers, Bob Devaney from Wyoming to Nebraska.

Where would I have gone? Who knows at this point, but as I pointed out there were lots of chances, and if I had taken one of those opportunities, I'm sure I could have enjoyed six or seven more years as an active and successful coach.

There are two things that can happen if you stay in one spot too long. You'll get fired, or you'll get hemorrhoids, or both. And both are occupational hazards. But capitalizing on opportunity hasn't always been a long suit of the Irish.

I once had an assistant coach who developed a bad case of hemorrhoids and required surgery. Now, I've often wondered if coaches develop that malady because so many folks are snapping at him all the time, or whether all of it is from nervous tension. At any rate, I went to the hospital to try and cheer him up. It was just a couple of days after his operation and he was pretty irritable, so I spent only a couple of minutes with him. When I came back two or three days later he was in much better spirits and antsy to get out of the hospital. He also was disturbed at his nurse. She was one of those "we" nurses, always saying, "Now, we're going to take our temperature" and, "Did we have our bath this morning?" and, "Did we get a good night's sleep?" and, "Did we enjoy our breakfast?" and, "Have we taken our medication?" and, "Did we have our enema yet?"

Well, she just drove him up the wall, so one morning he figured out a way to get even with this character. She roared into the room with two things on a tray—one was a glass of apple juice, and the other was a bottle in which he was to leave a urine specimen.

He knew the specimen bottle had been sterilized, so he poured the apple juice into that container. No more than fifteen minutes passed when the nurse came charging back into the room asking, "Did we have our apple juice?" and, "Did we leave our specimen?" He nodded, then she picked up the specimen bottle containing the apple juice and said, "My, we're a bit cloudy today aren't we?"

Right then and there he grabbed the bottle back from her. "Yes, we are," he said. "Maybe we oughta run that through one more time." With that, he gulped down the contents.

Like I pointed out, we Irish not only are noted for enjoying life to its fullest, but for procrastinating and for blowing opportunities. One of my favorite stories—and one that perfectly illustrates this trait—concerns Patty Hogan. The little Irishman decided one day to take a tour of the local brewery. As he was wandering about the catwalk, he fell into a 30,000-gallon vat of Guinness Ale and was drowned. The manager of the brewery ordered some workers to retrieve Patty's body, and he assumed the unhappy task of going down to inform the widow Hogan of the tragedy. He walked the three or four blocks to the Hogan house, then as gently as he could, informed Mrs. Hogan that as of that very minute, she was a widow.

"Poor Pat," she cried, "he couldn't swim a lick. The poor man never had a chance."

"Oh, no," said the manager, "Patty had several chances when he came out to pee."

Regrets? Sure, a ton of them. Mainly, I regret that we didn't win every single game because that's what it's all about. I regret that I didn't please everyone, that I didn't have time to go all the places and see all the people I wanted to see. I regret that we missed out on some great prospects because I would have enjoyed the association with them, whether or not they would have benefited from my coaching.

But it's been mostly fun. I wouldn't trade my experiences

for anyone else's I've ever known. I grew to hate recruiting, but we still managed to do it successfully. I cursed the polls at times, but I always wanted to be on top of them. Trite as it may sound, football is a great game and I'm proud to be a part of it. It was all worth it—even the walking away from it. I need television and I need my football clinics and my speeches and my public appearances, and I need people to walk up to me in restaurants and recognize me, because I cannot divorce myself from something that has been such a major portion of my life. If it weren't for football, I'd be Hugh Daugherty and no one would ever have heard of "Duffy."

When I resigned, members of the Spartan football team wrote me individual letters and presented a book in which everyone wrote something. I'll always treasure that. But the thing I treasure most is a letter from my daughter, Dree. My wife, Francie, and I have been fortunate in that our children, Dree and Danny, managed to keep their heads on straight through some difficult times. Just after I quit, Dree wrote this letter:

"Dear Mother and Daddy,

"People seem to be very sympathetic towards your resigning, Daddy. It seems that many people were concerned about how I would react. Pam's parents called her and were quite concerned about how I would take this. After they realized that I reacted favorably, they were much at ease.

"I am glad you did resign, Daddy. It seems as if sometimes the headaches outweigh the pleasures, and besides, there is much more to living than football and there are experiences to feel that even the two of you haven't accomplished yet. The world is here to explore, and to grow closer to God, and there is a lot left untouched. Soon you will have the time, and I pray you have the soul.

"I have grown more from being the daughter of a famous football coach than I think any other education could have given me. The keen sense of fair competition has enkindled my spirit from the time before I knew what competition was. I think that is why I am here at Stanford, why I have high goals, high ideals. Man must strive to be the best that he can, with whatever talents God has given him whether they be a team full of All-Americans or a team full of short, slow players; an ability to get along with other people, to laugh, to love.

"Competition makes striving for abstract goals more concrete, easier to grasp. I learned that to be a success is to be the best that you can, in whatever you do. And through football, I learned that to be good, you must work with other people, trusting them and fulfilling your role to your highest ability. By not being the daughter of a football coach, how would I have learned so graphically that not everything you read or hear may be precisely true? That it is imperative to learn both sides of an argument before passing judgment? How would I have learned except you are my parents, that some people are selfish and will try to hurt you by any means? That we must still love them and not hurt them back?

"I learned, too, how to accept defeat and not brood over it, but look optimistically toward the future. You have taught me to be an eternal optimist by accepting failure then planning ahead for success. And I have learned how to laugh by being your daughter, and learning the intrinsic value of a smile . . . how to be happy, and to make others happy. And love comes from loving others, and dedicating yourself to other people.

"I want to thank you for being my parents. And don't ever regret the fact that our family life was somewhat different from other families. We have experienced more together than they could ever realize.

"Love and tanti baci,

Dree."

Now, I really couldn't ask for anything else, could I?